Fully Human-Fully Divine

Fully Human-Fully Divine

Integral Dynamic Monotheism,
A Meeting Point Between the
Vedic Vision and the Vision of Christ

JOHN MARTIN SAHAJANANDA

Foreword by Swami Veetamohananda

PARTRIDGE
A Penguin Random House Company

To order additional copies of this book, contact
Partridge India
000 800 10062 62
www.partridgepublishing.com/india
orders.india@partridgepublishing.com

CONTENTS

FOREWORD

Who am I? Whence have I come? Whither am I going? These remain man's eternal questions. John Martin Sahajananda evokes the question "Who am I to you?" posed by Jesus to his disciples. The philosophical section of the Vedas has dealt with these questions in detail. The Seers of the Vedas discovered the eternal unity of existence which holds in its embrace 'all that has come to be'. Reality includes super-human, human, and sub-human beings. Reality pervades the entire Universe. It forms the inmost essence of all created beings, and yet transcends all. This Reality called Brahman is the indestructible Spirit in man.

Brahman is both a-cosmic or transcendental, and cosmic or phenomenal. The Vedas accept the empirical reality of the phenomenal universe and multiplicity of creatures. The attributeless, non-active Spirit cannot be the Creator. It cannot be the object of prayer and worship. But man is eager to know the Creator of the Universe. Man is the victim of fear, frustration, and suffering. He has a necessity for a Personal God who is benign and compassionate, and to whom he can lift up his hands for succor in times of stress and trial.

These needs are fulfilled by the Vedic conception of Saguna Brahman—who is the Creator, Preserver, and the Destroyer of the Universe. His love for creatures knows no bounds. He is the all-forgiving Father, the compassionate Mother.

Vedic Scientists called the first principle Brahman. Then through observing the changing phenomena of the Universe in man, understood him as Atman. Atman: the Reality, Intelligence, and Consciousness, which directly intuited is seen to animate the body, the sense organs and the mind.

The method of experimentation, observation, and verification, as well as the collection of facts applied by the Vedic Seers is very illuminating for the present day world too. Identification with Brahman and Atman is what is called Immortality-Self-Realization according to Advaita Vedanta (Non dualistic-School). The dualistic School of Vedanta regards souls as parts of God or as separate from God. But all admit the soul's immortality and its eventual perfection.

The Oneness of existence, the non-duality of the Godhead, and the harmony of all faiths are tenets of the eternal religion which is followed by the people of India. An individual is evaluated by his inherent worth and not by the colour of his skin, social position or economic rank. The Oneness of existence is the spiritual basis of this Santana Dharma (Eternal Rule or Law). By hurting another one hurts oneself. By loving others one loves oneself. These are all very much stressed in the Vedanta philosophy. The Oneness of existence includes all created beings—organic or inorganic. "Truth is One: Sages call it by various names" (Rig Veda).

Man is both Self and non-Self—this describes Vedanta. The Self is, in Reality, pure Existence, Consciousness, and absolute Bliss. The non-Self or apparent man is said to be the identification of the Self with the body, mind and sense organs. This identified, apparent man is subject to birth, death; experiences pleasure and pain. Thus man is a mixture of deity and dust. The Real and the apparent dwell in the same body.

The scientific analysis of the individual self (which we call non-Self) reveals five sheaths:

1 Annamaya Kosha—gross physical sheath which consists of flesh, bone, blood and other substances. This sheath depends upon food for its existence. It endures as long as it can assimilate nourishment. It was non-existent before birth. It lasts only a short period. Its virtues, such as strength, beauty are ephemeral. It changes its nature and hence it is not the Real Self.

2 Pranamaya Kosha—Within the physical sheath it is seen as an expression of Prana. Prana is the manifestation of the universal vital force. It is this Cosmic energy that sustains the physical sheath. This energy enables the created being to inhale (air), exhale, move, adapt to changing situations etc. It is through this sheath that one experiences hunger and thirst and engages

in various physical activities. The Real man (the Soul) cannot be measured by any of these aspects.

3   Mano-Maya Kosha—(Mind sheath)—Reactions, thinking, doubting, creating distinctions, etc, are all faculties of the mind. The various desires created by the mind result in suffering and bondage. The same mind which expresses itself as 'ego', when it is transformed into pure ego, leads man to liberation.

4   Vijnanamaya Kosha—(Sheath of Intellect) It is finer and even deeper within man. To come to certainty the Self uses the intellect—The intellect is extremely effulgent and closer to the Supreme Self. When the intelligence is purified, it shines, unites with the Atman (Self).

5   Anandamaya Kosha—The sheath of bliss through which one experiences varying degrees of happiness. This happiness, however, is not the bliss of Infinity (Brahman), since like other sheaths, this sheath experiences changes. The goal of Vedanta is to obtain complete freedom and be Bliss Absolute itself.

The five sheaths are all modifications of matter. With understanding and experience the illusory feelings disappear and the individual becomes Infinity itself. John Martin explains it very interestingly and in detail in this book.

Vedantins regard Jesus as a true Son of God, a true expression of Infinity. Sri Ramakrishna, whom all of India adores, used to listen to readings from the Bible. The divine teachings and the sublime personality of Sri Isa (this is how Jesus is known in India) readily inspired Ramakrishna's spiritual longing. The Son of the Mother (Sri Ramakrishna) was full of fond thoughts of the loving Son of the Father.

Sri Ramakrishna was resting in the garden house of a neighbour in Dakshineswar. His attention was forcibly drawn to a colourful image of the Madonna and Child on the wall. Suddenly the picture blazed forth with a heavenly radiance. Sri Ramakrishna felt the rays piercing his heart. The thought of Christ obsessed him for days. On the fourth day of this vision, Sri Ramakrishna saw a radiant figure with a fair complexion, large subtly luminous eyes, and flattened Semitic nose, strolling through the grove by the Ganges. He fixed his wondrous gaze on Ramakrishna. Within Ramakrishna resounded:-'Behold the Christ, who shed his heart's blood for the redemption of the World— Behold the Christ, who suffered a sea of anguish for the love of men. It is he, the Master Yogi who is eternally in union with God. It is Jesus, love incarnate!'

The two Supreme Lovers of God embraced, and merged into each other. Ramakrishna kept this vision of Christ fresh and vivid all his life. He used to burn incense before the image of Christ every day. He revered Christ as an Avatar of the divine.

For Vedantins, Jesus is the ideal for pure love, for renunciation, sacrifice and service to be practiced in their lives. This ideal is understood firstly by the cross. For Vedanta, the cross symbolizes the Infinite. This is explained in an Upanishad: Reality appeared to the Devas, to the Deities, as a column. The Gods wanted to measure it to know more about it. One of them went to the top and the other dug at its base, but both were unable to measure it. This shows us that the cross is nothing more than the symbol of the Infinite, this is how it is perceived. The horizontal represents its influence in the world of manifestation. Jesus was crucified on the cross, which symbolizes how the spiritual aspirant immerses himself in this Ocean of Infinity.

When one identifies with something other than this Reality, there is separation, division, identification and suffering. In the manifest world, we are attached to everything, identified with each of our sheaths, to each of our functions . . . This suffering is portrayed as the crucifixion of Jesus on the cross. It is not because of sins that we are crucified. There is an episode in the life of Jesus where a prostitute was brought before him to be judged. The usual custom was to condemn the sinner to stoning. Jesus said: "Let those who have never sinned, throw the first stone." Everyone went away. Then Jesus said to the person: "Go and sin no more." He meant that everyone should try to be pure, to live life in that consciousness of purity.

Jesus as the Ideal to be followed can secondly be understood through the concept of an afterlife. Jesus was born in the Jewish tradition where there is a notion of life after death. That is why he said: "After death, one enters Heaven or Hell." The concept of eternal sin or original sin has grown later. In Reality it is not because of the original sin that one remains forever in Hell. Jesus wanted to show that for every sinner there is the possibility of becoming a saint.

The third aspect of the life of Jesus is the ideal of renunciation, service and love. He loved the world, even people who insulted him or persecuted him. This is why he said on the cross: "O Father, forgive them for they do not know what they do."

Jesus has been the ideal both for renunciates and for laymen, as was Ramakrishna. He showed everyone how to live a righteous life. Why do Vedantins worship Christ? What sort of ideal is to be found in his personality? It is neither imagination, nor superstition, nor an appropriation of an aspect of another religion. There is no distinction of religion or belief. That is why Jesus is worshiped in the Ramakrishna Mission. December 24th is the day when Swami Vivekananda and his brother disciples glorified Jesus all night in the house of Swami Premananda. They did not know that it was December 24th and all night Swami Vivekananda spoke of renunciation and service of Jesus. He then made the resolution to live the life of a monk. All this shows that there is a deep connection and reverence for Jesus, not something superficial or imitated, within the tradition of the Ramakrishna Mission.

Swami Vivekananda would also talk of seeing God in others and especially in the poor. To the question how can we see God? Swamiji would answer: "No man can actually see God except through His human manifestations." He says in Lectures on practical Vedanta—Bhakti Yoga: "if we try to see God otherwise, we make of Him a horrible caricature and we believe it is not less than the original . . . as long as we are men, we cannot conceive Him greater than man. The day will come when we will exceed our human nature and we will know Him as he is. But as long as we are men we must worship Him in man as a man." And during a speech in India he said: "Worship Shiva in the poor, in the sick and in the weak . . ."

In his book John Martin speaks of this experience of pure Love, which is daily practiced in Ramakrishna ashrams as it is practiced in the Christian monasteries. The Mission has had the privilege of spreading the spiritual and cultural ideals of India directly and also indirectly through various activities, illustrating the central teaching of Sri Ramakrishna that all religions are expressions of the Truth. Centres have been created to provide both opportunities and places to allow real contacts between people professing different faiths, through public celebrations and meetings, through courses or in various publications. In India, these contacts have been facilitated by the presence of 180 libraries with large collections of books and magazines. In many places, reading rooms have been opened to the public. Colleges provide specialized education in the study of Sanskrit. The many Ramakrishna Vedanta Centres in the world have published very reasonably priced books dealing with religious subjects, and also magazines in many languages. In Centres outside India, the work is focused mainly on courses, lectures, meditation and spiritual retreats.

In these times of "isms," attended by selfishness with all its accompanying issues, John Martin's book makes bridges, as did Henri Le Saux and Bede Griffiths before him, showing new openings for constructive dialogue and experience. These are precious writings, and living and dynamic examples of Divinization to be followed, without restrictions, without barriers and without limits.

Swami Veetamohananda, Gretz, December 2013

INTRODUCTION

The two important questions that the human mind always asks are: 'who we are' and 'how we have to live our life in this world of time and space or what is the meaning and purpose of our life'. Every religion and every philosophy try to answer these questions. Today we can divide spiritual traditions into two categories: the Prophetic Tradition and the Wisdom Tradition. These two traditions tried to answer these two questions. There are three important answers given to the first question: 1. we are ultimately one with the Divine 2. We are the manifestations of God and 3. We are creatures of God. As per the purpose of our human existence some emphasize on Moksha or liberation and some on the love of God and the love of neighbour. It seems to me that the truth is somewhere in the integration of all the aspects not excluding one or the other. The wisdom tradition seems to focus on our divine nature and Moksha or liberation, which is realizing our oneness with God, as the supreme goal of life; whereas the prophetic tradition focuses on our human nature and the love of God manifesting in the love of neighbour as the goal of life. Both seem to be unsatisfactory. The first tends to focus on the beyond and the second on the below. It is the integration of these two aspects that gives us a satisfactory vision. The Vedic Tradition had proposed this integral vision and Jesus Christ also had proposed this integral vision but somehow these visions have been diluted and fragmented. This book, Integral Dynamic Monotheism, tries to rediscover their original vision.

This book has two important parts. The first Part is titled as 'Integral Dynamic Monotheism' and the second Part as 'what is Truth?' This is not completely a new book. A chapter with the title 'Integral Dynamic Monotheism' is published in my previous book What is Truth? published by ISPCK, New Delhi, 2012. The second part, What is Truth?, is also one of the important chapters in the same book with the title 'Bearing Witness to the Truth'. I have developed extensively the theme of Integral Dynamic Monotheism hence the need for a new book. There are two reasons for including the chapter 'Bearing Witness to the Truth' in this book as part 2. Firstly this chapter also deals with the theme of dialogue between the Vedic Vision and the Vision of Christ. Secondly the copies of 'What is Truth?' are completely sold out.

The title of the book is Fully Human-Fully Divine:*Integral Dynamic Monotheism: a Meeting Point between the Vedic Vision and the Vision of Christ.* Integral Dynamic Monotheism is not an exclusive vision but an inclusive vision that tries to integrate the Prophetic Monotheism with the Hindu Monotheism. It is called *Monotheism* because it affirms that there is only one God, one infinite Reality. It is based on the fundamental truth of the

Vedic tradition which affirmed *Ekam sat vipra bahuthi vadanti*, there is only one infinite Reality but sages call it by many names. The same truth of one infinite reality is affirmed in the Biblical Tradition also. We read in Prophet Isaiah, *'I am Yahweh and there is no other God except me'* (Isaiah.45.5a). It is called *dynamic* because human relationship with that one God is not static but a dynamic process of ascending and descending in which human beings can experience God in different ways but cannot be reduced into any one way. It is growing from the dualistic relationship with God to the non-dualistic relationship and then returning back to the dualistic relationship. It is *integral* because it does not exclude any spiritual path but integrates every spiritual path that helps human beings to grow in divine-human relationship and human-human relationship. The sub title is: *a Meeting Point between the Vedic Vision and the Vision of Christ.* It is chosen with a purpose. Hinduism is not one religion but a congregation of many religions with many belief systems within the label of Hinduism. They are all different interpretations based on the Vedas, the Upanishads and the Bhagavat Gita. The Vedic sages had an integral vision of spiritual understanding which can give possibility to interpret into many systems of theology or philosophy. Hence I prefer to base on the Vedic Vision and not on any particular system of Hinduism. In the same way Christianity is not one religion but a congregation many religions or belief systems. Today there are thousands of Christian denominations in the world under the label of Christianity, each one having its own specific beliefs. They are all interpretations based on the Old Testament and the New Testament. Jesus Christ had an integral vision of spiritual life. Unfortunately his vision has been diluted and fragmented. Hence I would like to focus on the Vision of Christ rather than on any particular Christian belief.

In the first Part 1 I explore different belief systems of Prophetic Monotheism and Hindu Monotheism and show that each system is very important but it needs to integrate the other systems also. I tried to show that that Vedic Vision cannot be identified with any one Hindu system but it can be described as Integral Dynamic Monotheism. In the same way I tried to show that Jesus' vision can be identified with any one Christian belief but can be described as Integral Dynamic Monotheism. Hence the Integral Dynamic Monotheism is a meeting point between the Vedic Vision and the Vision of Christ. The whole point is who is a human being? Some systems emphasize the human nature of human beings and others emphasize on the divine nature. Some emphasize on internal purification and some emphasize on the love of neighbour and the social transformation. The truth is to bring these two together. Human beings are divine in one pole and human in another pole. They need to grow into the love of God as much as they need to grow in the love of neighbour. The Vedic seers and Jesus Christ seem to present this integral view.

In the Part 2 I tried to show the similarities between the spiritual evolution in the Vedic Tradition and in the Biblical Tradition. I tried to show that the Upanishadic tradition had a very integral view of Truth which is the union of the Infinite and the finite. The Chandogya Upanishad defines Satyam, Truth, as sat-ti-yam. Sat means infinite, ti means finite and yam means union.

Satyam, Truth is the union of the infinite and the finite. Jesus Christ presents similar view of the Truth. He is understood as fully human and fully divine. In him the infinite and the finite are united. There are some differences between these two traditions but these differences are marginal. An open-hearted dialogue can bring these two visions together. If that happens then more than half of the world would be united. What an exciting thing to hope for?

On the cover page we have the symbols of OM and the CROSS shaking hands. The OM in Hinduism is the symbol of the fullness of Truth. It is the symbol of the unity of the infinite and the finite. There are four circles. Three are dotted circles representing a-sat, relative truths and one thick lined circle representing sat, the divine, the infinite Truth or the absolute Truth. The Mandukya Upanishad describes the three relative truths as waking consciousness, dreaming consciousness and the deep sleep consciousness. The fourth level is the awakened consciousness of Brahman or Atman. We need to grow from the relative truths to the absolute Truth, from finite to the infinite. Once we discover the Infinite then the finite is also seen as the manifestation of the infinite: that is fullness this is also fullness (Purnamadah purnamidam). There is no conflict between the infinite and the finite, sat and a-sat. Hence OM is Sathyam, the Truth.

The CROSS is the symbol of Christ and it is the symbol of the fullness of Truth. It has also four circles. Three are dotted circles and one is thick lined circle. The three dotted circles represent the three finite aspects of Jesus Christ, the physical Jesus, Jesus the Jew and

Jesus, the Son of God. The fourth line represents the divinity of Christ. Jesus Christ is one with God. Once Jesus had discovered his divine nature, he integrated his human nature also. He is fully divine and fully human. He is the Satyam, the Truth. He is the union of the infinite and the finite. Hence the symbol OM represents the Vedic Vision and the symbol Cross represents the Vision of Christ. They are shaking hands. They have found a common ground in their vision.

I would like to thank Swami Veetamohananda, Vedanta Centre, Gretz, France, for accepting my request and writing Foreword for this book. In spite of his busy schedule he was able to spare his time, read the material and wrote a wonderful Foreword. I am very grateful to him. I am also grateful to Nadine who coordinated between me and Swamiji. I am also grateful to Madam Yvonne Lanners who read the draft and gave me valuable suggestions. Most of the material for this book I have taken from the internet and synthesized hence I could cite the references. I hope I do not offend anyone. I would like to thank also Fr. George and my community members who wholeheartedly supported to publish this book as they have always done before. Finally I dedicate this book to my parents whose physical marriage of a Hindu and a Christian has borne fruit in me into a Hindu-Christian Spiritual marriage.

Br. John Martin, Saccidananda Ashram, Shantivanam, Thannirpalli, Tamilnadu, South India-639107.

19.2.2014.

CHAPTER 1

INTEGRAL DYNAMIC MONOTHEISM

INTEGRAL DYNAMIC MONOTHEISM—1

All philosophies, all ideologies, all scriptures, all religions and all prophets and sages tell us two important things: who we are and how we ought to live our lives in the world of time and space. The way persons live their life, I believe, will depend largely on their self-identity—on who or what they think they are. I'd like to explore with you some powerful teachings about who we are that have influenced the lives of millions. I want to show that they all have something of value to offer us. The mystery we call 'God' undoubtedly has many different aspects for us to discover and experience if we are ready to drop our narrow concepts and go forward with an open heart and mind. I'll confine myself here to the major types of religious teaching that have shaped for centuries, and still shape today, our understanding of who or what we are and how we should live.

These days it's common for theologians to divide religions into two major overall categories (though not in an absolute sense)—the Wisdom Tradition and the Prophetic Tradition. Religions like Hinduism, Buddhism, Jainism and Taoism belong to the Wisdom Tradition. These religions deal with some common elements such as: karma, samsara, reincarnation and spiritual enlightenment. Religions like Judaism, Christianity, Islam and Baha'i' belong to the Prophetic Tradition.[1] These religions are also called monotheistic religions as they teach the belief in one God. In our exploration, we will focus our reflection on the monotheistic religions and Hinduism.

Prophetic Monotheism

According to traditional Judaism, God is the creator and human beings are creatures of God. God creates the cosmos and human beings out of nothing. There's a gulf between God and his creation—an essential difference between God and humankind, and, coincidentally, between all of God's creatures, human or otherwise. According to this tradition, no one can see God face to face. God is the liberator and saviour. He guides his people through the prophets. He reveals his will through the commandments. The Torah reveals the will of God and people have to follow it. To obey the Torah is to obey God. One has to submit one's will and intellect to the will of God and one has to be faithful and loyal to God. Jews consider themselves to be specially chosen by God. According to Judaism, they're

---

[1] Sikhismis also a monotheistic religion.

expected to live a moral life according to the will of God.

Traditional Christianity also considers God to be the creator and human beings are creatures of God. There's an essential difference between God and humankind. God revealed his will through the prophets in the First Covenant or Old Testament and he revealed his final will in the person of Jesus Christ. Most Christian churches believe and teach that the Bible, and especially the New Testament, is the inspired word of God and that to be guided by the Bible is to be guided by God. Jesus Christ is the only Son of God. He's the incarnation of the second person of the Holy Trinity. He is the only way, the truth, the life. One has to believe in Jesus as the only Son of God and become a Christian to be saved. Some Christians insist only on believing in Jesus as the savior for redemption while others insist not only on believing in Jesus, but on living a moral life and doing good works. If one lives a good life, they believe, one will go to heaven and if one lives a bad life, one will go to hell after death.

According to traditional Islam, God is the creator and human beings are creatures of God. There's an essential difference between God and his creation. God revealed his will through the prophets in the Old Testament and through Jesus, but he revealed his final will in the Koran (or, Qur'an) through the prophet, Muhammad. Hence the Koran is the final word of God and the prophet, Muhammad, is the last prophet. According to Islam, God did not reveal so much of himself but rather revealed the Koran in which he tells human beings what they should do and what they should not do. The Koran is considered as the eternal word of God dictated to the prophet, Muhammad. Submission to the will of God—revealed in the Koran—is necessary for salvation. To obey the Koran is to obey God. If one lives a moral life according to the Koran, one will go to heaven and if one does not live a moral life, then one will go to hell after one's death

According to these three religions, God is the creator and human beings are creatures of God. A significant difference between Judaism, Islam and Christianity lies in their attitude towards Jesus and the Trinity. Jews and Muslims do not believe that God is triune. They think the notion of Trinity violates the unity of God. They do not believe that Jesus is the second person of the Trinity. Jews and Muslims do not believe that Jesus is the only Son of God and that he is the only way, the truth and the life. They believe that Jesus was a human being like any other human being. They think of him as a messenger of God or reformer of Judaism. If he called himself 'the Son of God', they maintain, it was only in a metaphorical sense and that everyone is a son or daughter of God.

These three religions are called monotheistic religions because their adherents believe that there's only one God and this one God is the creator of the universe. Their general teaching is that God created this universe out of nothing[2], and, that there is an essential difference between God and his creation . . . which includes us.

---

2   Whatever may be the meaning intended by it.

In Christianity, an exception to this belief is made for Jesus. Jesus, it is believed, is not a creature of God but an incarnation of God. He is fully human and fully divine. There is an essential difference between Jesus and other human beings.

INTEGRAL DYNAMIC MONOTHEISM-2

Hindu Monotheism

The expression Hindu monotheism may surprise some. In general Hinduism is described as monism, non-dualism, pantheism and polytheism. But one has to be aware that according to Hinduism, there's only one God or absolute Reality (monotheism). Ekam Eva advitiyam, there is only one being; no second one. Ekam sat vipra bahuthi vadanti, Self-existent being or God is one but sages call it by many names. But this God is not the creator but manifests everything that is known. Hinduism does not propose the theory of 'creation out of nothing'. This is the basic difference between prophetic monotheism and Hindu monotheism. Hinduism is not one religion but a congregatioin of many relgions. There are many belief systems within the label of Hinduism but all call themselves Hindus. There are six important theological positions in Hinduism. These positions are based on the interpretations given to the teachings of the Upanishads, the Bhagavad-Gita, and the Brahma Sutras—the sacred scriptures of Hinduism. The Upanishads belong to the period of the 5th century before Jesus and the Bhagavad-Gita belongs to the time around the 1st century before or after Jesus.[3] These scriptures did not propose any one theological system. The systems came later. The fundamental question of these systems is the relationship between God and the universe, or, God and humankind. In prophetic monotheism, this question seems to have been resolved with the theory of creation out of nothing. Since Hindu monotheism does not accept this solution, it needs to propose different solutions.

Advaita—Non-Duality

The first Hindu philosophical system we shall consider is called Advaita, a system of non-duality proposed by Sankara in the 8th century after Jesus. According to Sankara, God (Brahman) alone is eternal (Brahma sathyam). The universe, he taught, has only the appearance of reality (Jagat Mithyam). The illusory nature of the manifest world, in this system, is also known by the often used word: Maya. Ultimately, the human soul (jivatman), he taught, is identical with God (Jeevo Brahmaiva na parah). This can be explained with the analogy of water (representing God) and ice (representing human beings). Ice, as we know, comes from water and melts back to water. It could be said, that a block of ice does not have an existence independent of water. Also, the block of ice always has a beginning and an end—it comes and goes, as we see with glaciers or icebergs.

---

[3] There can be diferent views on it.

The iceberg (or ice cube) is essentially one with the water in which it floats, though it is functionally different. The ice does not become water. It is water. But it is not aware that it is water. Because it is solid, it imagines, let us say, that it is an object like a stone. If this were the case, we could say it was in a state of ignorance. It would then need to free itself from this ignorance and realize that it is essentially water or God. Growing out of this ignorance is the purpose of life for all human beings. All the negative manifestations or evil come from ignorance. Sankara proposed the way of wisdom known as jnana marga. The paths of devotion (bhakti) and action (karma) can prepare the way, but jnana is the ultimate one in his view. Sankara taught that ignorance can be removed only through wisdom or understanding and not by devotion or action, as they are not the opposite of ignorance. For Sankara, God or Brahman is nirguna, without qualities. Brahman is impersonal. Human beings are essentially one with God, but they are ignorant of this truth. They need to awaken from ignorance and realize the liberating truth about themselves. According to him, ultimately every one of us can say aham Brahmasmi, 'I am Brahman, God and I are one.' A person who realizes this truth while alive is called jivan muktha—liberated while alive. Some consider Sankara to be a monist in the sense that the world is an illusion. Others consider him to be a non-dualist in the sense that the world is not an illusion but unreal, finite. According to the second view God and the universe are not two independent or separate realities. God is sat, self-existent and creation is a-sat whose existence depends on sat. I would hold the second view.

Visistaadvaita—Qualified Non-Dualism

The second Hindu system we are considering is called Visistaadvaita, a system of qualified non-dualism, proposed by Ramanuja, in the 11th century after Jesus. He disagreed with Sankara's position regarding the nature of God, the universe and humankind. For Ramanuja, as with Sankara, God (Brahman) alone is eternal (sathyam). But according to him, God is not nirguna, without qualities, but saguna, with qualities. Ramanuja taught that God is personal. Brahman is qualified by the sentient and non-sentient beings. They constitute inseparable parts of God. The universe and our world (Jagat) is the manifestation of Brahman (not a mere appearance, mithya, as with Sankara). The universe is not created by God, but rather is seen as an emanation from God. God is the material and instrumental cause of creation. We are part of God but not identical with God. There is an essential subtle difference between God and us. Ramanuja saw the universe and humankind as the 'body' of God. The relationship between God and the universe, he taught, is like soul and body, or the body and the hair that grows on and from the body. God and the universe are inseparable. The material world is not an illusion, mithya or Maya. Maya, he teaches, is the creative power of God through which he manifests the world and everything in it.

If we go back to the analogy of water and ice, Brahman, according to this system, is water; ice is the universe. The universe is not an illusion. It is the manifestation of Brahman. It is the body of Brahman. But there is a subtle difference between God and the universe, which includes humankind—it is not identical with Brahman. Ramanuja proposed the way of devotion, bhakti marga. One has to surrender to God, he taught, through devotion or faith—to God's will—and one finds peace and joy in this surrender. Human soul is not identical with God. No one can say, 'God and I are one.' Jnana, wisdom and karma, action can be expressions of bhakti. For him, a personal relationship with God is very important. If a human soul were one with God, then no personal relationship is possible. He taught that we can have a personal relationship with God in one or more modes such as: father and child, lover and beloved, protector and protected; physician and patient, owner and the owned, sustainer and sustained, supporter and dependent, sun and lotus and many more.

Ultimate liberation, Ramanuja taught, happens only after the death of the physical body. Some Western theologians suspect him of being a pantheist. But this view may not be correct since he holds that there is a subtle essential difference between God and the universe in general or humankind in particular. From the Sun come many rays, but one cannot say that every ray is a Sun. There is only one Sun (God) and the universe is its manifestation.

Dvaita—Duality

The third position in the Hinduism we are considering is called Dvaita, a system of duality, proposed by Madhva, in the 12th century after Jesus. He disagreed with both Sankara and Ramanuja regarding the nature of God, creation and human souls and proposed dualism. Madhva would agree with Sankara and Ramanuja that God alone is eternal (sathyam). He identifies Brahman with Vishnu. The universe is essentially different form God. The material world is not an illusion (Sankara). It is not the manifestation of God (Ramanuja). It is not created by God. The universe, he taught, was there from the beginning, as if it is eternal, though essentially different from God. Human beings, Madhva taught, are essentially different from God. There is a gulf between God, the world and humankind. The immeasurable power of Lord Vishnu is seen as the efficient cause of the universe and the primordial matter or prakrti is the material cause of the universe. God is personal and has many qualities, saguna. The human soul is essentially different from God. This position keeps human beings somewhat distant from God and strengthens the relationship between them.

Madhva proposed the path of devotion, bhakti marga, and good works, karma marga. One needs to surrender to God through devotion and do good works. It is the Lord who performs actions—energizing the soul from within—awarding the results to the soul, but he, the Lord, is no touched by it. According to Madhva, we are more or less creatures of God (though he may not like to use the word 'creatures', in the sense of being created out of nothing). We are essentially different from him and remain so after this life. We are urged to come closer to God through devotion, but we can never merge with him. Liberation (bliss) is awarded to us according to our actions at the end of our spiritual practice, which would be after our death.

Dvaitadvaita-duality-non-duality:

The fourth system is Dvaitadvaita proposed by Nimbarka in 12th. A.D. It means duality and non-duality at the same time. According to him the categories of existence are three, i.e., cit (conscious beings), acit (unconscious beings), and Brahman or Isvara. These three are equally real and co-eternal realities. Brahman is the Controller (niyantr), the cit, the enjoyer (bhoktr) and the acit, the object enjoyed (bhogya). Cit and acit are different from Brahman, in the sense that they have attributes and capacities, which are different from those of Brahman. Brahman is independent and exists by Himself, while cit and acit have existence dependent upon Him. At the same time cit and acit are not different from Brahman, because they cannot exist independently of Him. Difference means a kind of existence which is separate but dependent, while non-difference means impossibility of independent existence. Nimbarka says that animate and inanimate world exist in a subtle form in the various capacities (saktis) which belong to Brahman in its natural condition. Brahman is the material cause of the universe in the sense that Brahman brings the subtle rudiments into the gross form by manifesting these capacities. This position is called parinamavada. For Nimbarka the highest object of worship is Krishna and His consort Radha, attended by thousands of gopis, or cowherdesses, of the celestial Vrindavan. Devotion, according to Nimbarka, consists in Prapatti, or self-surrender.

He proposed five methods to salvation: the first one is ritual actions performed conscientiously in a proper spirit according to one's caste (Varna) and phase (asrama) of life. The second one is knowledge as an independent means of salvation but only for those who are inclined to spiritual study and reflection. The third one is meditation which has three types: first is meditation on the Lord as the Inner Controller of the sentient; second one is meditation on the Lord as the Inner Controller of the non-sentient; the third one is, for those who are inclined to it, meditation on Lord Himself, as different from the sentient and non-sentient. The fourth way is devotion and self-surrender to God as Shri Radha Krishna which is available to all people irrespective of caste and stage of life. The fifth one is devotion and self-surrender to guru. It is best realized as a part of self-surrender and not as an independent means, although it can be so. This system somehow tries to synthesize the three previous systems: advaita, visistaadvaita and dvaita.

Acintya Bedabeda-Inconceivable difference and non-difference:

The fifth position on divine-human relationship is called acintya bedabeda, inconceivable difference and non-difference. It was proposed by Sri Caitanya Mahaprabhu in the 15th century A.D. This is very similar to the previous position of dvaitadvaita but simplified. This system disagrees with Sankara that the human soul is essentially one with God. It also disagrees with Madhva that human souls are utterly different from God. It proposes that individual souls (jivas) and the material world are simultaneously one with and different to God. They are one in the sense that they are separated parts of God. If God were gold individual souls would also be gold. That is oneness of quality. But God is great and human souls are minute. In that way they are different. So the difference is in quantity and not in quality. Krishna is the Supreme absolute Truth endowed with all energies and he is the ocean of love. Pure devotion is the practice of individual souls and pure love of Krishna is the ultimate goal. If the individual souls are under the influence of matter they are bound. If they are free from the influence of matter they are liberated. Krishna is the only lovable blessing to be received. Both God and His creatures are living entities, though God is the chief. The difference between the two is that God maintains all the other living entities. Individual souls are maintained and God is the maintainer. God is independent and individual souls are dependent. HDG.A.C. Bhakti Vedanta Swami, the great proponent of this philosophy in the modern times says:

"The part is never equal to the whole. That is an axiomatic truth. So it is a wrong conception to try to become equal to God. The Maya Vadis (Non-dualists) are trying to become God, but that is impossible. Let them try to become godly. Godly means 'servant of God'. Being a servant of the Supreme will make them perfect". *The Vaisnava philosophy teaches that we can remain in our natural position but act as a servant of God. That is perfect. But if the servant tries to become the master, that is artificial.*

But he also sees the possibility of equality in a higher state of experience. This system proposes the path of bhakti—surrender and master-servant relationship with God. They also use mantras like Hare Rama and Hare Krishna and bridal dance, which take one to the mystical experience with Krishna. It seems that Caitanya took initiation from Sankara sampradaya, he took philosophy from the tradition of Ramanuja and his disciples are considered Brahma Sampradaya of Madhva. His system is a kind of marriage of these three systems like dvaitadvaita but somewhat simplified.

Suddadvaita-pure non-dualism:

The sixth system is called Purified-Non-dualism, proposed by Vallaba(1479-1531). According to him in 'essence' there is no difference between the individual soul and God, like sparks to the fire. God is the whole and the individual soul is its part. The individual soul is not Brahman clouded by the force of avidya but is itself Brahman but with one attribute, ananda, rendered imperceptible. (According to Sankara's advaita, an individual soul is Brahman clouded with the force of avidya). The soul is both a doer and enjoyer. It is atomic in size, but pervades the whole body through its essence of intelligence (like sandalwood makes its presence felt through its scent even if sandalwood can't be seen).

Unlike Advaita, the world of Maya is not regarded as unreal, since Maya is nothing else than a power of Isvara. He is not only the creator of the universe but is the universe itself. Vallaba cites the Brihadaranyaka Upanishad account, that Brahman desired to become many, and he became the multitude of individual souls and the world. Although Brahman is not known, He is known when He manifests Himself through the world.

Bhakti is the means of salvation, though Jnana is also useful. Karmas precede knowledge of the Supreme and are present even when this knowledge is gained. The liberated prsons involve in all actions even after liberation. The highest goal is not Mukti or liberation, but rather eternal service of Krishna and participation along with His activities in His Divine abode of Vrindavan. Vallaba distinguishes the transcendent consciousness of Brahman as Purushottama. He lays a great stress on a life of unconditional love and devotion towards God.

In the system of Suddadvaita, God is one without the second one. He is the only Ultimate Reality or the only category. Every other thing has proceeded from it at the time of creation, is non-different from it during creation and merges into it at the time of dissolution. The two other categories namely the animate souls and the inanimate objects are respectively its parts and modifications. The animate souls are its parts because they retain to some extent the essential qualities thereof namely consciousness and joy. The inanimate objects are its modification because the above said qualities are absent therein.

Before we conclude our exposition of Hindu philosophical systems it is also useful to see the contributions of Sri Ramakrishna, Swami Vivekananda and Sri Aurobindo who have great influence on Hindu thinking.

Sri Ramakrishna-Unity of Hindu Religions:

Sri Ramakrishna(1836-1886) did not identify himself with any particular sect of Hinduism but accepted Hinduism as a whole. He showed that Dualism, Non dualism and other schools of Hindu philosophy represent different stages of the integral experience of Reality, and that the various Hindu Deities are different aspects of one supreme God-head. His message has brought about a great deal of harmony among the Hindu sects, and Sri Ramakrishna himself has become the symbol of the unity of Hindu religion. It should be noted that Sri Ramakrishna recognized the differences among religions but showed that, in spite of these differences, they lead to the same Ultimate Goal. This is the meaning of his famous maxim, Yato mat, tato path, "As many faiths, so many paths". It seems that Vivekananda, in one of his lectures after speaking about Ramanuja, Caitanya and Sankara, said of his master: : "One had a great head, the other a large heart, and the time was ripe for one to be born, the embodiment of both this head and heart; the time was ripe for one to be born, who in one body will have the brilliant intellect of Shankara and the wonderfully expansive, infinite heart of Caitanya; one who in every sect will see the same spirit working, the same God, one who would see God in every being, one whose heart would weep for the poor, for the weak, for the outcaste".

Ramakrishna was initiated into different sects of Hinduism, Islam and Christianity. It seems he had the vision of Christ. Ramakrishna believed that bhakti marga and karma marga are the ways which take one to advaitic experience. Even after reaching advaitic experience, nirvikalpa Samadhi, he kept on praying to a personal God, because he had a mission on earth and he had to set an example for the world to follow. Ramakrishna is considered to be an avatar, incarnation of God, not any person who had realized God. Swami Vivekananda was the foremost disciple of Sri Ramakrishna who brought the message of Vedanta to the west.

Swami Vivekananda-Sanathana Dharma:

Swami Vivekananda preferred to call Hinduism as Vedanta. He saw Vedanta as the ultimate religion and the destiny of every human being. He called it Sanathana dharma, eternal universal religion which can serve as the ground of all religions. All religions are expressions of that one eternal religion. The foundation of Vedanta is: *Ekam sat vipra bahuthi vadanti*, Self-Existent Being(God) is one, and sages call it by various names. His Vedantic teaching can be summed up in four principles: God as Pure Spirit alone abides; the world of diversity is the manifestation of God in time and space; the individual soul and God as the Supreme Soul are non-different in essence; and realization of this identity alone can confer liberation and put an end to all the sorrows and sufferings of life.

The removal of ignorance and the manifestation of inner divinity leading to God realization are achieved through Yoga. There are four main Yogas or margas: Jnana Yoga (Yoga of Knowledge); Bhakti Yoga (Yoga of Devotion); Raja Yoga (Yoga of Meditation); Karma Yoga (Yoga of

Work). According to Swami Vivekananda each yoga is an independent means of realizing God. But since each Yoga involves the cultivation of one of the faculties such as reason, feeling or will, a combination of all the four Yogas is necessary for the development of a balanced, 'fully functioning' personality. It is this synthesis of Yogas that Swami Vivekananda regarded as the ideal of Ramakrishna Math and Mission. This ideal finds expression in the emblem of the Ramakrishna mission.

Ignorance of one's true nature makes one weak and this weakness is the cause of immorality, evil and suffering in life. Knowledge of one's true self makes one strong and helps to overcome weakness and live a virtuous life. It helps to actualize one's divine potentialities. The purpose of education is to help human beings actualize their divine potentiality. Since creation is the manifestation of God, all work is sacred. So every work should be done with devotion. Vivekananda followed his master who said 'to serve Jiva as Shiva' (*Shiva Jnane Jiva Seva*). Vivekananda said: 'He who sees Shiva in the poor, in the weak and the diseased really worships Shiva; and . . . with him Shiva is more pleased than with the man who sees him only in temples.' It was Vivekananda who coined the word daridra-narayana (God in the poor) to refer to the poor. This service done as worship helps the person who is served and helps spiritually the person who serves.

Sri Aurobindo-divinizing the matter:

The teaching of Sri Aurobindo is based on the discovery of the Vedic sages that there is one absolute reality,Brahman or Saccidananda. All beings have their foundation in that one Reality. It reflects in every being as the divine spark. Due to ignorance this divine spark feels imprisoned in the body and mind complex. It is possible to remove this veil of ignorance by certain psychological discipline and become aware of the true Self, the Divinity within us. Evolution is the method by which the divine spark liberates itself from the matter and realizes its oneness with the Source. Consciousness appears in the unconscious state and once having appeared it is self-impelled to grow higher and higher and at the same time to enlarge and develop towards a greater and greater perfection. Appearance of life is the first step that moves into the mind level. But evolution is not finished with reaching the mind. It awaits a release into something greater, a consciousness which is spiritual and super mental. A breakthrough has to take place in the consciousness by which mind has to change into the higher principle. The method to do this is the ancient psychological discipline and practice of Yoga. In the past, the focus has been to withdraw from the world and disappear into the infinite Self but Sri Aurobindo taught that the goal of spiritual evolution is not to disappear into the Higher Self but to bring down the higher spirit into the world and replace the mind's ignorance with the Higher Consciousness. This transformed consciousness will be an instrument of the Higher Self and makes it possible for the human beings to grow out of their still animal humanity into a divine race.

The psychological discipline of Yoga can be used to that end by opening all the parts of the being to a conversion or transformation through the descent and working of the higher still concealed supra mental principle. He proposed the path of Integral Yoga which is a combination of the principles of the old systems, the way of knowledge through the mind's discernment between Reality and the appearance, the heart's way of devotion, love and surrender and the way of works turning the will away from motives of self-interest to the Truth and the service of a greater Reality than the ego. For the whole being has to be trained so that it can respond and be transformed when the higher spirit manifests. It is not the object of Sri Aurobindo to develop any religion or to amalgamate the older religions or to found any new religion—for any of these positions would lead away from his central purpose. The one aim of his Yoga is an inner self-development by which each one who follows it can in time discover the One Self in all and to evolve to a higher consciousness than the mental, to a spiritual and supramental consciousness which will transform and divinize human nature and matter.[4]

INTEGRAL DYNAMIC MONOTHEISM-3

(Some Observations)

HereI would lik some observations on the above Prophetic and Hindu Monotheisms.

Prophetic Monotheism:

The prophetic Monotheism affirms the existence of One God who is a transcendent mystery. The cosmos

---

[4]   This synthesis is taken from the interent.

and all living beings are created by God. Creation is essentially different from God. Creation is good. Human beings are very good. There is a positive purpose of creation. Human beings have the vocation to live in harmony with the will of God. It is to be fruitful and multiply. It emphasizes the personal relationship with God. The aspect of community is emphasized and God relates with people as a group. God actively involves himself with the people as a saviour and liberator. The love of God and the love of neighbour are the two pillars of prophetic monotheism. There is also emphasis on moral life and justice in human relationships and compassion and concern for the poor and the needy in society. But the prophetic monotheism reduces human beings to mere creatures of God. It closes the door to the realization of being sons or daughters of God and finally realizing oneness with God. The theory of creation out of nothing, which seems to satisfy inquisitive human mind, is not a very liberating theory. It blocks the spiritual evolution of human consciousness. Unless Prophetic monotheism goes beyond this theory of 'creation out of nothing' it cannot evolve officially into higher divine-human relationships. The uniqueness of prophetic religions is the emphasis on the love of God and the love of neighbour. God actively involves with the people as a protector, savior, liberator and consoler. God leads people in time space. Human history has a menaing and purpose.

Jesus' experience of God goes beyond the traditional Jewish experience of God. He claimed to be the Son of God and to be one with God. For Jesus God was not his creator but his Father or Source. He was ultimately one with God. "The Fahter and I are one" he declared. His religious authorities considered his statements blasphemous. He was in conflict both with the religious and political authorities and he met a violent death. St. Paul took human beings from creatures of God to adopted sons and daughters of God (Jesus Christ being the natural son of God) though he fell short of proposing equality with Christ. Christian mystics took human consciousness beyond dualistic relationship with God into mutual indwelling and even into oneness with God. Meister Eckhart used more of a non-dualistic language. While commenting on the beatitude 'Blessed are the poor in Spirit' he said that a poor person is one who ultimately says that 'God and I are one. The Christian mystics also had difficulties with the hierarchy. Many were condemned as heretics. Meister Eckhart also was under inquisition.

The mystical tradition of Judaism, Kabala, takes human consciousness beyond the traditional dualistic relationship between God and human beings into a relationship in which human consciousness empties itself completely in such a way that it becomes a vehicle of divine consciousness. We can say that it takes human consciousness beyond dualistic relationship with God. But it is seen as an esoteric path accessible only to few. It tends to become a very exclusive and individualistic path. Orthodox Jews do not accept this mystical path.

Sufism, the mystical tradition of Islam goes as well beyond the traditional dualistic relationship with God. It recognizes one central truth, the unity of being, wahdat. All phenomena are manifestations of a single reality, which is Truth or God, al-Haq. The essence of Truth or God is devoid of any form and quality and therefore remains un-manifest. Yet it is inseparable from every form and phenomena either material or spiritual. It implies that every phenomenon is an aspect of Truth, but at the same time it is false to attribute real existence to it. The main goal of Sufis is to let go of all notions of duality (and therefore of individual self also), and realize the divine unity which is considered to be the truth. Human beings are not separate from the divine. Sufism is not satisfied with mere intellectual understanding of truth but strives for experiential knowledge of it. It is identifying with the truth where the knower and the known are transcended. It proposes a spiritual path of dis-identification in which human consciousness empties itself completely in such a way that only God remains. The main focus is that everything is grounded in the unity of God. But this also tends to be very esoteric and individualistic path, having very little sense of community and concern for the poor, the needy and for social transformation. Traditional Islam does not recognize it and considers Sufism to be heretical. Some Sufi mystics, like al Halaj, were even killed for their un-orthodox mystical views.

So we can say that in the Prophetic monotheism there are different levels of divine-human relationship, even though the traditional currents of these religions may not accept or recognize them. We can find three views about a human being. The traditional view is that human beings are creatures of God. In the mystical traditions they are manifestations of God or sons and daughters of God and then the possibility is opened of being one with God. But the basic truth is that there is only one God. Hence they are monotheistic religions.

Hindu Monothiesm:

All theological systems in Hinduism affirm the existence of one absolute reality: *ekam sat vipra bahuthi vadanti*, Self-existent Being (God) is one but sages call it by many names. Ekam Eva advitiyam—There is only one (God) without a second one. In that sense Hinduism is monotheistic. It differs from prophetic monotheism regarding the relationship between God and creation and the identity of human beings. It does not accept the theory of creation out of nothing[5]. Different schools of Hindu Monotheism propose different solutions. The advaita system of Sankara affirms the existence of one God, one eternal reality, Brahman. Human soul is none other than Brahman. We can call his position as non-dualistic monotheism. The position of Sankara on the nature of the world is very ambiguous. If he really means that the manifest universe is an illusion, then it could be said that we live a purposeless creation and purposeless human existence. If he means that the material world, in the sense of names and forms, is not eternal, not infinite then there is some meaning to the world and human existence. The names and forms are not eternal, but what is within the names and forms is eternal. In that sense the world is also divine in its

---

[5]   The relationship between God and creation remains a mystery any attempt to identify it creates more problems than solving it.

essence just as human beings are also essentially one with the divine in their essence. This position does not mean that a human soul becomes God. There is no human soul becoming God. We can use the analogy of infinite space as the symbol God and the space within the walls is the symbol of human soul. The walls are the symbol of names and forms. If the walls are taken away the space within the walls is one with the infinite space. It does not become infinite space but it is infinite space conditioned by the four walls. That is what Sankara means when he says that a human soul is none other than Brahman. Sankara gave some meaning and purpose to the world in the vyavaharika level. Only in the ultimate level, paramarthika, is the world seen to be illusory.

Sankara is not satisfied with anything but our divine oneness. The entire focus is to realize our divinity and then everything comes to an end. We can say that the greatest contribution of Sankara is to open the human consciousness to the realization of its oneness with that one eternal reality. This also has been the focus of the Upanishad sages. This was the vision of a spiritual eagle. This vision was necessary during his time as the spirituality at that time was very much based on ritualism, superstition and sentimentalism. But this was done at the cost of discounting our humanity. Human existence and relationships seem to have little or no significance in the light of his teachings. His position doesn't give any positive role to the universe and human beings in the world of time and space. Human beings are like prisoners of war in this world. They should try to escape from this prison of samsara-birth and death—as early as possible.

Ramanuja tried to correct this extreme position and give some meaning and purpose to creation and human relationships. According him there is only one God and creation and human beings are manifestations of that one God. We can call his position as Qualified non-dualistic monotheism. The contribution of Ramanuja is that he accorded us the dignity of being divine manifestations and of having divine kinship. He has given importance to the heart and loving relationships but it was done at the cost of denying our oneness with God. He does not give much space for our human frailties. His focus is on our divine son-ship and daughter-ship. His position that God is qualified by the creation and human souls, somehow, limits the transcendence of God. Meanwhile Ramanuja holds that Brahman is the material and instrumental cause of the material universe and human souls. In that sense they are essentially one with Brahman though functionally may be different like water and ice. If this is so, what then would prevent us from being merged with Brahman, just as melting ice is finally merged with the water in which it floats? It seems that there is some contradiction in his proposition. Ramanuja denies the possibility of our oneness with God and he also does not take into account our human limitations. The path of surrender he proposes may not be possible to every human condition. Human beings are conditioned in different ways and they are in different levels. Everyone might not be able to surrender as he proposed.

Madhva tried to bring God to the level of ordinary human beings with all their characteristics and limitations. He says that there are two eternal Realities: God is and Creation. But God is greater than creation. Human beings are less than God and they can never be equal to God. We can call his position as Dualistic Monotheism. It was the need of the time but it was done at the cost of denying their innate kinship with God and their oneness with the divine. Madhva holds that creation is completely different from God. He also holds that the manifest world has no beginning as if it also is eternal. How can there be two eternal realities? Does this imply that there are two 'Gods'? This is what really his system *duality* means. Sankara melts our human consciousness in the ocean of divine. Ramanuja keeps it at the level of an ice berg and Madhva bring it to the level of solid earth boarding the ocean but separate from the ocean.

Nimbarka was a man of peace and reconciliation. He tried to bring a kind of reconciliation among these three systems and proposed dvaitadvaita. He agrees with Sankara that the human soul is one with Brahman. In that sense he is an advaitin. He agrees with Ramanuja that Brahman is the material and instrumental cause of creation. In this sense he is a visistaadvaitin and he also agrees with Madhva that creation and human souls are co-eternal with Brahman. In this sense he is a dvaitin. He holds that creation and human souls are at the same time different and non-different from Brahman. The questions one might ask to Nimbarka are: how can there be three co-eternal realities? Does it not imply three Gods? If they are co-eternal how can Brahman be the material cause of the universe? We can admire his good will for reconciliation and harmony but his proposition seems to be little artificial. His proposal of five ways to salvation i.e. ritualistic action, knowledge, meditation, self-surrender and devotion to the Guru is very inclusive and has universal validity. This can be his original contribution. His proposition of highest worship of Krishna with Gopis in Vrindavan is very materialistic and does not correspond to the advaitic experience proposed by Sankara. He agrees with the advaita system that sentient beings and creation are ultimately nothing but Brahman. He also insists on the difference. They are not illusion. In this sense he differs with advaita. The difference is only in appearance. The relationship between Brahman and the universe is like a snake and a coil, between sun and its rays, between different stones and the earth. Just as the coil is nothing but a snake, the sun rays are nothing but Sun, different stones are nothing but earth. Yet the snake is different from the coil, the sun rays are different from the sun and the stones are different from the earth. So also Brahman and the universe are one but different because of their own peculiar natures and attributes. Sankara uses the image of rope and snake. Brahman is like rope and creation is like snake. People mistake the rope for the snake. When they see the rope the snake disappears. In this sense creation seems to be an illusion.

Nimbarka agrees with visistaadvaita but also differs from it. According to Ramanuja Brahman is qualified by sentient and non-sentient beings. They are part of his body. Brahman is the material and instrumental cause of the sentient and non-sentient beings so also for

Nimbarka Brahman is the material and instrumental cause of the universe. The difference is that for Nimbarka both the difference and non-difference are important whereas Ramanuja subordinates difference to non-difference. Ramanuja says that there is a subtle essential difference between Brahman and the universe where as for Nimbarka there is no difference between Brahman and the creation. This is the subtle difference between Ramanuja and Nimbarka. He agrees with the dvaita system of Madhva but also differs from it. Madhva says that creation and human souls are not created by God but they are eternal, though completely different from God. Nimbarka also says that the sentient beings (cit) and non-sentient beings are co eternal with God. In that sense Madhva and Nimbarka are similar. But Nimbarka says that sentient and non-sentient world exist in a subtle form in the various capacities (saktis) which belong to Brahman in its natural condition. Brahman is the material cause of the universe in the sense that Brahman brings the subtle rudiments into the gross form by manifesting these capacities. In this sense he differs from Madhva. Since he was trying to combine both dvaita and advaita his system is called dvaitadvaita. We can describe his system as Dualistic and Non-dualistic Monotheism.

Caitanya's(15 a.d.) vision, acintya bedabeda, is very much based on Nimbarka's vision of dvaitadvaita but he simplifies it. It is very much reconciling the position of advaita and dvaita. Advaita asserts that the individual soul and God are one and the same; dvaita says that the individual soul and God are eternally separate. **Acinthya bedabeda affirms that there is only one**

God. Creation and human souls are different from God and at the same time not different. They are one in quality but different in quantity. This position is inconceivable (acintya) to human mind. Creation has a separate existence from God and at the same time it is never separate from God. God exercises his power over his creatures through his energies. This relationship can be like spider and the web, the earth and the plant and the hair in the human body. Pure devotion is the practice of individual souls and pure love of Krishna is the ultimate goal. The contribution of Caitanya is putting fire to the heart. It is the awakening of pure love and devotion to God. Caitanya danced in ecstasy. But his proposition of self-surrender as the only way, excluding knowledge and action, and conceiving God only as Krishna and master-servant relationship with God as the only possibility is very limiting and can become exclusive. His position can be described as Acintya Bedabeda Monotheism.

The Suddadvaita system of Vallaba sees every manifestation as divine. We can describe it as Pure Monotheism. It is possible that if a person sees the creation and human souls with the eyes of the divine then there is only divine manifestation. There can be an essential oneness of God and creation. If the human consciousness is not in that position then there is a stage of ignorance. Vallaba does not give place to ignorance. If the human soul is not in ignorance then what is the necessity of any spiritual path?

What is the source of negativity and evil? If everything is Brahman from where does evil come? His emphasis on eternal service to Krishna in his activities in the abode of Vrindavan and not on mukthi orliberation is very original. His proposal of Bhakthi as the main means of salvation and rendering second place to jnana can be very limiting.

Sri Ramakrishna did not propose any new system but embraced all the systems of Hinduism as different ways of experience of God. He believed the existence of one God (Monothiesm), who is the source of all religions and all spiritual paths. His ultimate vision is advaita—experience of oneness with God. He was a man of peace and reconciliation. He is a healer of divisions. He was initiated not only into different sects of Hinduism but also into Christianity and Islam. He saw truth in every religion. Yato mat, tato path, "As many faiths, so many paths' can be the contribution of Sri Ramakrishna. He also showed love for the poor, the weak and the outcast. His was a spirit of reconciliation, inclusiveness and compassion. He brought tremendous healing to the quarreling Hindu sects and had the heart of embracing all spiritual paths. He did not have a systematic explanation of his truth like Shankara or Ramanuja. It was reserved to his prominent disciple Swami Vivekananda. Ramakrishna spoke from his personal intuitive experience of God. We can describe his vision as Integral Non-Dualisitc Monotheism.

Swami Vivekananda calls his vision as Vedanta, Sanathana Dharma. He affirms the existing of one pure and eternal reality(monotheism). Human soul and God are one in essence. In these two aspects he agrees with Sankara. For him Creation is not an illusion but

the manifestation of God. In this sense he disagrees
with Sankara and agrees with Ramanuja and Nimbarka
and Vallaba. Realization of this oneness of human soul
with God is the goal of life and end of human misery
and suffering. His proposal of Integral Yoga, which
gives equal place to all important paths of Hinduism is
something original. His consideration that all religions
as manifestations of Sanathana Dharma, the eternal
religion, very bold and also unifying. His emphasis
on the realization of one's divine nature places human
beings above religions or belief strucutres. He also
integrated service to the poor in his vision which is
based on his advaitic vision of oneness of reality. He
also advocated the ufliptment of the lower classes in the
society and eradicating the difference between the rich
and the poor, even though it did not affect the society
at large. This aspect was the original contribution of
Swami Vivekananda in comparison to the other systems
which neglect this aspect. It began with Sri Ramakrishna
and found a strong expression in Swami Vivekananda's
vision. We can also call the vision of Swami Vivekananda
as Integral Non-Dualistic Monotheism

Sri Aurobindo adds his own original contribution to the
spiritual search of Indian sages. He bases his philosophy
on the one eternal Spirit (Monotheism) of which the
Indian sages constantly speak. He sees this Spirit being
entangled with matter and evolving back to its source.
He sees the spiritual journey as a process of evolution
from natural life of the body to the Super mind, super
consciousness. He felt the need of a break-through
from the rational mind to the super mind. He felt
that the Indian sages were very much concerned only

ascending to the source without returning back. Hence he proposed the descent of the higher power which will not only liberate the spirit from the clutches of matter but also enters into the matter and divinizes all aspects of human life including the body in such way that the body becomes immortal, deathless. He advocated integral yoga, like Swami Vivekananda, which is the combination of jnana yoga, bhakti yoga, karma yoga and raja yoga, as a means of facilitating this evolution. He did not propose any new religion but advocated that each individual should concentrate on his /her own spiritual evolution. We can say that the original contribution of Sri Aurobindo was: to look at spiritual life as evolution; a mutation or breakthrough from mind to the super mind: and the descent of the spirit into the matter in order to divinize it. The main comment we can make about Aurobindo's vision is a question: why does the Spirit entangle with matter? It seems there is no satisfying answer for that. His path is a very individualistic path. He did not emphasize very much on the love of neighbour. We need to remember that before his entry into a serious spiritual path he was very much involved in the Indian struggle for freedom. We can also call his vision as Integral Transfroming Monothiesm.

When we look at the spiritual evolution of Hinduism we discover that it has reached its climax in the Upanishads, which affirmed that the Atman, the ground of human consiocusness is one with Brahman, the ground of the universe. Sankara (8 A.D) gave a systematic explanation of this vision in his advaitic system in which he emphasized divinity of the human soul. In Ramanuja (11 cent. A.D) it came down to qualified non-dualism. He brought down human soul to be a part of God but not one with God. Madhva (12 A.D), in his dualistic system, built a gulf between God and human soul. He holds that the human soul is not one with God, not a part of God, but essentially different from God. It is more like a creature of God in the traditional Prophetic religions. Nimbarka (15 A.D.) takes it up again to advaitic experience without denying dvaita. He tried to reconcile the positions of Sankara, Ramanuja and Madhva. Caitanya (15 A.D) held the position that the human soul is both non-different and different from God in an inconceivable way. Vallaba (1479-1531) takes it up again to Pure-non-dualism in essence but different in manifestation. Sri Ramakrishna (1836-1886) proposes an inclusive vision that embraces all experiences and all religions but focusing on non-dualistic experience of God. Swami Vivekananda(1863-1902) proposes that the human soul in essence is one with God. He advocated advaita as the ultimate destiny of our spiritual evolution but integrated all spiritual paths and gave them an equal place. He added service to the poor to his vision. Sri Aurobindo(1872-1950) looks at spiritual life as an evolution, which is not only an ascending journey but also descending. It is divinizing the human consciousness and matter. What we notice is that the human consciousness is oscilating from the divine to the human and from human to the divine.

All are Monotheistic

When we look at all these above philosophical and theological systems both in the Prophetic tradition and

Hindu tradition we discover that they all affirm that there is only one God, one absolute Reality. In this sense they are all monotheistic. The only difference among them is the status of creation and human beings in relationship with that one God. We can say that there are different types of monotheisms:

1. The Prophetic Monotheism of Judaism, Christianity and Islam;

2. The Non-dualistic Monotheism of Sankara;

3. The Qualified Non-dualistic Monotheism of Ramanuja;

4. The Dualistic Monotheism of Madhava;

5. The Dualistic-Nondualistic Monotheism of Nimbarka

6. The Inconceivable Difference and non-difference Monotheism of Caitanya;

7. The Pure Non-dualsitic Monotheism of Vallaba;

8. The Integral Monotheism of Sri Ramakrishna and Swami Vivekananda;

9. The Transforming Integral Monotheism of Sri Aurobindo;

Basing on the status of of creation and human beings we can divide these monotheisms into five main types of Monotheisms.

1. **Creation and Human Souls are essentially different from God:** The prophetic religions of Judaism, Christianity and Islam come under this category. These three prophetic religions say that there is only one God and that creation and human beings are created by God (out of nothing) and so there is an essential difference between God, creation and human souls. One experience of Jesus also belongs to this level. He said:my Father is greater than me

2. **Creation and Human Souls are eternal but essentially different from God:** The Dvaita system of Hiinduism comes under this category. It says that creation and human souls are not created but eternal but they are essentially different and inferior to God. They are more creatures of God, even though it does not say so.

3. **Creation and Human Souls are eternal. They are essentially one with God and also different from God:** The Dvaitaadvaita system of Hinduism comes under this category. It says that creation and human souls are one with God at one level and also different from God at another level. There are one at the source and different in the manifestation.

4. **Creation and Human Souls are manifestations of God**: The Visistaadviata system of Hinduism, the Kabbala system of Judaism, Christian Mystics, the Sufi system of Islam, Acinthya Bedabeda system of Caitanya and one experience of Jesus Christ belong to this understanding. Jesus Christ is not a creature of God but incarnation of God. They all say that there is only one God and creation and human souls are not created by God but manifestations of God.

5. **Creation and Human Souls are essentially one with God**:,the advaita system of Sankara, Dvaitaadvaita system of Nimbarka, the Suddaadvaita system of Vallaba, Sri Ramkrishna, Swami Vivekananda, Some of the Christian Mystcis and Sri Aurobindo come under this category. One experience of Jesus Christ also comes under this category when he said that the Father and he were one.

The Meaning of Salvation

In the three prophetic religions, Judaism, Christianity and Islam, salvation is after death to be in the presence of God. There is no possibility of being saved while a person is still alive in this world. It will be decided only after one's death whether a person goes to hell or heaven. May be it is possible in the mystical traditions of these religions to have a deeper communion with

God but this is not considered to be salvation while alive, like Jeevanmuktha[6] in Hinduism.

In Hindu tradition salvation or mukthi or moksha or liberation is seen as freedom from birth and death. To be born in this world is seen as a consequence of one's actions in the previous life. Almost all Hindu theological systems hold this view except Vallaba for whom Mukti or liberation is not the highest goal but rather eternal service to Krishna and participation along with His activities in His Divine abode of Vrindavan.

The ways to liberation are karma marga, bhakti marga, Jnana marga and Raja marga. Sankara insists on Jnana, Ramanuja on Bhakthi, Madhva on Bhakti and Karma, Nimbarka on all of them, Caitanya on Bhakti, Vallaba also on Bhakti, Sri Ramakrishna embraces all, Swami Vivekananda calls his way an integral way which embraces all margas as equal means of liberation and adds service to the poor. Sri Aurobindo also proposes an Integral way just like Swami Vivekananda but adds the descending of the divine energy to transform the human consciousness and the matter.

What is the purpose of creation?

What we find in all these Hindu systems is that there is no satisfying purpose of creation and human relationships. In general to be born in this world is seen as something negative and one should try to escape

---

[6] Jeevanmuktha means experience of liberation while a person is still alive.

from this world of samsara—birth and death—as early possible. The goal of one's life is moksha or liberation which is freedom from birth and death. There is an over emphasis on the vertical relationship with God and very little emphasis on the horizontal level of human relationships and the social transformation. Spiritual life tends to be very individualistic. Even though Swami Vivekananda speaks of serving the poor it is only to purify oneself. Service is seen for one's own salvation and also for the welfare of the world.

All these systems of Hinduism are based on the interpretation of the Upanishads and the Bhagavat Gita. What is the philosophical system that these two scriptures propose or advocate? It seems to me that these two Scriptures give possibility for many interpretations but their vision cannot be reduced into any one particular system.

INTEGRAL DYNAMIC MONOTHEISM-4

Integral Dynamic Monotheism of the Upanishads and the Bhagavat Gita

Our next question is: what is the vision of the Upanishads and the Bhagavat Gita? Is it advaita, visistaadvaita, dvaita, dvaitadvaita, acintya bedabeda, Suddadvaita, Sri Ramakrishna, Swami Vivekananda and Sri Aurobindo? It seems to me that we cannot place the Upanishad sages and the Bhagavat Gita into any of these categories. They can give the possibility of different interpretations but they can never be put into any rigid system. I would like to call the vision of the

Upanishads and the Bhagavat Gita as Integral Dynamic Monotheism. The foundation of the Upanishadic truth is the affirmation of Rig Veda: *ekam sat vipra bahuthi vadanti* and *ekam eva advitiyam*: Self-Existent Being or God is one but sages call it by many names and there is only one ultimate reality without a second one. It is affirming one God or one absolute Reality. It is monotheism. The climax of the Vedic journey and the discovery of the Upanishad sages is the oneness of Atman with Brahman. Even though each Upanishad has a unique approach to the Truth, the essential teaching of all the Upanishads is the same: the oneness or identity of Atman with Brahman. Atman is the ground of the human consciousness and Brahman is the ground of the universe. When we discover the ground of our human consciousness, the Atman, we also discover the ground of the universe, Brahman, because they are one and the same. Atman is not the human soul. It is the ground of the human soul, it is God.

The Chandogya Upanishad and the Mandukya Upanishad present the evolution of human consciousness in four levels of consciousness. The first level is called "waking consciousness," the second level is called "dreaming consciousness," the third is "deep-sleep consciousness," and the fourth one is turiya and can be described as "awakened consciousness."

The Waking consciousness is a way of life in which we identify with our physical body and live to satisfy only our physical desires and ambitions. Everything that we do is intended to satisfy the needs of our body and of the senses. Here our identity is with the body: I am my body. We can describe this level as "individual mind" or "individual consciousness." Here truth is individualistic. A person says: I (body, the individual) am the way, the truth and the life. It is a very materialistic view. If it is a spiritual vision then it is very individualistic spiritual vision.

The Dreaming consciousness is a way of life in which we have ideals to follow and ideal persons to imitate. In general these ideals and ideal persons are taken from the past. We are inspired by the great personalities and their ideals from the past and wish to imitate them and follow them. We place our body at the service of these ideals and ideal persons. The present receives its identity from the past. We can call this consciousness "collective mind" or "collective consciousness." This collective consciousness unites us with some persons and divides us from others. This consciousness has a boundary to protect and also a possible mission to expand. Here a person's life is guided by the moral code of a particular religion. Truth at this level is an ideal, a belief structure. At this level, religions or belief structures are the way, the truth and the life.

The Deep sleep consciousness is a way of life in which a person transcends ideals and ideal persons and enters into the direct contact with eternity. It means the past comes to an end. When past comes to an end, future also comes to an end. The present becomes a vehicle of eternity. It becomes original and creative. Here a person's identity is 'I am'. We can call this consciousness universal consciousness. Here a person identifies with all and lives for all. It is all embracing consciousness. It has no boundaries to protect and has no mission to expand. It invites everyone to transcend collective consciousness and enter into the universal consciousness.

The fourth level is the awakened consciousness where a person realizes that his or her ground of consciousness is Atman or Brahman. This is the non-dual consciousness or unitary consciousness. It is all embracing divine consciousness.

According to these two Upanishads the human consciousness grows from the individual consciousness to the collective consciousness, from the collective consciousness into the universal consciousness and from the universal its goes into divine consciousness, where it realizes that Brahman, the ground of the universe is one with Atman, the ground of human consciousness. It does not become one with Brahman because it is already Brahman. **In this sense we can say that the divine-human relationships are not static but dynamic**. There is not only an ascending journey but also a descending journey.

The Upanishads in general propose the path of wisdom and there is not much emphasis on devotion and action. The Svetasvathara Upanishad introduces the theme of Bhakti-devotion, submission to God and grace of God. It gives forms to the formless God. This Upanishad also presents God as the creator and sustainer of the universe. It mentions that God or Parama Purusha is shining in its glory beyond the darkness of ignorance or Tamas. God controls the material energies of the universe through his characteristic Maya, but God is not bound by his Maya as humans are, because he is its controller and is capable of giving salvation to human beings. The Isa Upanishad adds the necessity of action. Actions done in God bind not the soul of a human being, it declares. It also says that knowledge without action is insufficient and action, that does not come from wisdom, also can be binding. The sign of a liberated being is the union of wisdom and action.

The author of the Bhagavat Gita was a spiritual genius. He presents an inclusive vision in which there is a place for every spiritual path leading people to the one goal. Krishna tells Arjuna: "in whatever way people worship me in that way I accept their worship and bless them". This is a remarkable statement which gives freedom to everyone to worship God the way one wishes. In this way the Bhagavat Gita complements the vision of the Upanishads. It also gives emphasis on three important margas or paths: jnana, bhakthi and karma, wisdom, devotion and action. But the originality of the Bhagavat Gita is the marriage of wisdom and action in love. According to Gita Love is wisdom manifesting in action. Krishna is the symbol of wisdom and Arjuna is the symbol of action. They are in the same chariot. Krishna guides Arjuna and Arjuna acts according to Krishna. They love each other. Wisdom manifests in actions and actions come from wisdom. This is the great vision of the Bhagavat Gita. **This is an integral path or integral vision.**

Hence we can describe (not to define) the vision of the Upanishads and the Bhagavat Gita as **Integral Dynamic Monotheism**. It is Monotheism because it affirms that there is only one Absolute Reality or one God. It is Dynamic because human beings grow in their relationship with God. In the waking consciousness and dreaming consciousness human beings have a dualistic relationship with God. They experience distance between God and themselves. In the deep sleep consciousness they experience the indwelling presence of God. They will have a qualified non-dualistic experience of God. In the awakened consciousness they realize their oneness with God. Here they have the experience of non-duality, advaita. But this consciousness needs to return to the waking consciousness. In the process of this return to the waking consciousness the human beings experience dvaitadvaita or bedabeda relationships with God. In this sense Dynamic Monotheism embraces all the systems proposed in a dynamic growth. This Monotheism embraces all spiritual paths and practices that help human beings to grow in their relationship with God. It does not exclude any spiritual path. It is all inclusive. Isa Upanishad and the Gita introduce the necessity of action. Wisdom needs to manifest in action. Love is wisdom manifesting in action. Human consciousness needs to become the vehicle of the divine consciousness. Arjuna finally says to Krishna: I will do thy will. The predominant tendency of the Upanishad vision is to ascend to the higher level of consciousness. Realizing oneness with God is the ultimate purpose of life. There is neither emphasis on the descending of the spirit nor on the love of neighbour and social transformation. Sri Ramakrishna and Swami Vivekananda added the elements of loving actions to the poor. Sri Aurobindo adds the elements of profound conversion or breakthrough, the descending of the Spirit and divinization of human nature and matter. **Hence I would like to describe Hindu Monotheism as Integral Dynamic Monotheism**.

INTEGRAL DYNAMIC MONOTHEISM-5

The Spiritual Vision of Jesus Christ

In this section I would like to reflect on the spiritual vision of Jesus. The spiritual journey of Jesus took place in a different social, cultural, political and religious context in comparison with the Hindu spiritual journey. And yet we find some similarities in his spiritual journey and experience of God. The first question I would like to ask is whether Jesus Christ is a prophetic monotheist or a Hindu monotheist. Jesus reportedly made statements which do not fit within the popular versions of prophetic monotheism. He referred to God as his Father. He referred to himself as the Son of God. He said that he was in the Father and the Father in him. He said he came from the Father and would return to the Father. He also claimed that the Father (God) and he were one. His stated experiences of God do not fit within the present belief systems of prophetic monotheism. For Jesus, God wasn't his creator and he was not a creature. His origin, he reportedly said, was in eternity . . . eternal! Judaism and Islam reject his claims and consider them blasphemous. They think that his statements are metaphorical and not metaphysical. Christianity accepts his claims, but limits them to Jesus alone and holds that they are in no way applicable to others. The claims of Jesus seem very close to the non-dualistic and qualified non-dualistic systems of Hinduism. In fact, his statements make perfect sense to adherents of these two systems. In this regard, Jesus was more a Hindu monotheist than a prophetic monotheist! In non-dualism and qualified non-dualism, these claims aren't limited to any particular individual but are a possibility for every human being.

The second question that we are going to ask is: what is the concept of Jesus Christ regarding the relationship between God and creation, God and human beings? in which system can we place Jesus Christ? in advaita? Visistaadvaita? Dvaita? Dvaitadvaita? Acintya bedabeda? Suddadvaita? Is he Ramakrishna? Swami Vivekananda? Sri Aurobindo? Here we are dealing with this question retrospectively. These systems were not formally established during the time of Jesus. They were formulated many centuries later than Jesus Christ. But they do give us some tools to understand the experience of Jesus.

Jesus reportedly made three important statements: "my Father is greater than me," "I am in the Father and the Father is in me', and, "the Father and I are one." The first statement is in accordance with the dualistic system. God is the creator and Jesus is the creature. God is greater than him. The second statement is in accordance with the qualified non-dualistic system. Here, the relationship is much more intimate. It's not the relationship of creator and creature—it is the relationship of Father and Son. He is in God and God is in him. It is an experience of mutual indwelling. Still there is some distance between him and the Father. He is not the Father. The third statement is in accord with the non-dual system. Jesus Christ and God are one. There is no distance. There is no separation. If we take these positions all together, then it appears that Jesus is contradicting himself. If God is greater than him, then he cannot say, "I am in the Father and the Father is in me." If there is a distance between God and Jesus, then he cannot say that he and God are one. Jesus also said," Father, if it is possible take away this cup from me;but it is not my will let thy will be done",and "my God, my God, why have thou forsaken me?". When we listen to the statements of Jesus we discover that almost all the systems presented in the Hindu Tradition are found in his experience. We cannot place him exclusively into any system. He had his own unique experience of God.

I would like to propose that Jesus evolved in his relationship with God. In him we discover that there is an aspect of ascending and also an aspect of descending. Jesus said: no one has ascended to heaven except the son of man who descended from heaven. Jesus Christ had many important moments in his life. We can take four of them as turning points in his life, before his crucifixion, death and resurrection, like the ones we saw in Chandogya Upanishad and Mandukya Upanishad.

The first moment was his birth as a human being through his physical mother, Mary. She conceived him, nourished him, protected him in her physical womb and then gave birth to him as a human being. In that sense Jesus was a hundred percent human being. This was his waking consciousness.

The second moment was the day of his circumcision. On the eighth day of his birth Jesus was circumcised according to the Jewish tradition. With this Jesus became a Jew. He was not only a human being but also a Jew. He entered into the collective consciousness of Judaism. He lived like a Jew. He worshipped God like a Jew, he ate like a Jew and he spoke like a Jew. In that sense he was a hundred percent Jew. Judaism was his truth, his way and the model for his life. As a Jew he might have said that Judaism was his way, his truth and his life. He was in the dreaming consciousness of Judaism.

As he grew in his spiritual tradition he began to discover its limitations. Discovering the limitations of one's spiritual tradition is a sign of maturity and growth. The first limitation was that his religion, at that time, divided human beings into two: the Jews and the Gentiles. So there was a wall between the Jews and the Gentiles. The second limitation was that God was understood only as the God of the Jews and not of the Gentiles. There was again a wall between God and the Gentiles. The third limitation was that the external Law took the place of God and human beings were at the service of the Law, or religion. The fourth limitation was that God was a transcendent mystery inaccessible to human beings except through the mediation of the Prophets or the Commandments. The fifth limitation was that his religion created an exclusive collective consciousness thus becoming a source of enmity, conflict and violence.

This realization brought Jesus to the third important moment of his life which was his baptismal experience.

The baptismal experience of Jesus was a moment in which he came out of the womb of Judaism and entered into the universal presence of God. It was his spiritual rebirth. First he came out of the physical womb of his physical mother, Mary, and now he came out of his religious womb, Judaism. In this experience the wall between the Jews and the Gentiles was broken down and a new human being was born. It was the birth of a new human consciousness which was united with the whole of humanity and the whole of creation. This new human consciousness was neither a Jew nor a Gentile but the child of God or the Son of God. It was the birth of Universal Consciousness which embraced the whole of humanity and the whole of creation. In this experience the wall between God and the Gentiles was also broken down and God became the God of the whole of humanity and of creation and not just the God of the Jews. God was not only a transcendent mystery but also an indwelling presence, Emmanuel. The Spirit of God descended upon Jesus and God lived in him and he lived in God. Jesus said, 'I am in the Father and the Father is in me' (Jn.14.11). He also said: 'I am the way, the truth and the life. No one can come to the Father but through me" (Jn. 14.6-7).

This statement has to be understood in the context of the New Covenant that God promised to the Jewish people. God gave them Ten Commandments to regulate their lives. But their relationship with God was oscillating between faithfulness and unfaithfulness. It was a turbulent relationship. So God promised that he would make a New Covenant with the people in which he would write the Law in the hearts of the people so that everyone would follow the will of God without being told. (Cf.Jer.31.31-34). It is not really a New Covenant but we can call it 'eternal covenant' written in the heart of human beings when God creates them. In the first covenant God told people what they should and shouldn't do but in the New Covenant God tells who human beings are. That self-knowledge becomes the way, the truth and the life and human beings have to live from this inner wisdom and no more from the external commandments. We can speak of a quantum leap in the divine-human relationship. Here Jesus entered into the deep sleep consciousness.

The fourth important moment in the life of Jesus was when he grew one step further and realized that God and he were one. He declared: 'the Father and I are one'. This was the last stage of his ascending journey to God. Jesus Christ, not only entered into our original image and likeness of God, but went beyond that and discovered that he was one with God. St. John says, 'In the beginning was the word, the word was with God and the word was God' (Jn.1.1.). At this level Jesus' consciousness is one with God and the life he lives is the life of God. At this level God is the way, the truth and the life. This was his awakened consciousness. We can say that Jesus grew from the waking consciousness to dreaming consciousness, from dreaming consciousness to deep sleep consciousness and from there to awakened consciousness.

I suggest that Jesus began his spiritual journey with the consciousness of being a creature and experienced God as being greater than him according to his religious tradition. Then, at the moment of his baptism he went beyond that relationship and realized that he was not so much a creature but a son of God—a manifestation of God! Later, Jesus went beyond even this realization and became conscious, or saw, that he was inseparably one with the Father—with God. The gospels indicate though that he didn't remain pre-occupied with non-dual consciousness, but fluctuated between it and qualified non-dual consciousness and dualistic consciousness. We have seen above different types of monotheisms: the prophetic monotheism of Judaism, Christianity and Islam; the Hindu monotheism of Sankara, Ramanuja, Madhava, Nimbarka, Caitanya, Sri Ramakrishna, Swami Vivekananda, Sri Aurobindo. The experience of Jesus, recorded in the gospels, does not fit exclusively into any of these monotheisms. His experience of God is closer to the Integral Dynamic Monotheism of the Upanishads and the Bhagavat Gita but not completely identical with it. Jesus experience of God is not completely identical with the Vedic experience of God. Yet we can call Jesus' vision as Integral Dynamic Monotheism.

INTEGRAL DYNAMIC MONOTHEISM-6

The Integral Dynamic Monotheism of Jesus

Jesus described his experience of God as the kingdom of God. The kingdom of God is transforming our life into life of God and transforming our actions into actions of God. He invited everyone to search for the kingdom of God and live according to its vision. The similar word for 'the kingdom of God' in Hinduism would be Sanathana dharma, the eternal religion. I would like to describe the vision of Jesus Christ as Integral Dynamic Monotheism. This is very similar to the Integral Dynamic Monotheism(IDM) of the Upanishads and the Bahgavat Gita but it has its own uniqueness.

It is monotheism: It is monotheism because it affirms that there is only one God without a second one. In this monotheism, God alone is. God alone is eternal (sathyam and nithyam). God cannot be put into any human categories. He/She/It is absolutely independent, creative, timeless, peace and love. God is personal, impersonal, and at the same time, beyond these categories.

God is not an object or form but rather formless, like infinite space. Our concepts of God are like houses that we build within the space. The infinite space allows the building of houses according to the needs and capacities of human minds, but the space always transcends them. Our finite human mind can never build an adequate house to fill or accommodate the infinite space. God is the unconditioned space and systems (especially belief systems) are like conditioned space, within walls, as it were. Systems can never satisfy our deepest needs.

Creation (names and forms) is nothing less than a manifestation of God, and as such, is not illusory. It is not created by God 'out of nothing'. It is, however, unreal in the sense that it is not eternal and infinite. It is limited and finite. Creation, like all its constituents, has a beginning and an inevitable end. All forms are temporary. The universe is essentially one with God, but different in manifestation, like water and ice, energy and matter etc. Water and ice, as we have seen, are essentially one, but different in manifestation or functionally. Likewise, energy and matter are essentially one, but functionally different. We too, it could be said, are essentially one with God, but different in manifestation or functionally:

Human souls are reflections of God in the mirrors of Names and forms. When the reflection identifies with names and forms, it feels that it is finite and nothing more. However, when it looks to its source, it realizes it's oneness with God. All of us have the opportunity in this life to evolve or move beyond our present spiritual capacity and experience more deeply our essential oneness with God. The mystery we call 'God' undoubtedly has many different aspects for us to explore and experience if we will but drop our narrow concepts and go forward with an open heart and mind.

It is Integral: This monotheism which I am proposing integrates all the systems mentioned above and also other possible systems, but always transcends every system. God or Truth cannot be put into any system. It is essentially non-dualistic but functionally qualified non-dualistic and dualistic. We cannot fix it to any mode of experience. This monotheism does not exclude any mode of spirituality, but embraces all spiritual paths that help us to grow in our relationship with God, the Source of all, and with one another. Any spiritual path that helps human beings to grow in relationship with God is accepted. The spiritual paths of wisdom (jnana), devotion (bhakti) and action (karma) are not seen as exclusive, but mutually complementary.

It is Dynamic: The relationship between ourselves and God is not static but dynamic. It's a process of ascending and descending (or vice versa). It is like climbing a hill and coming down again (or vice versa). We could, for instance, grow in our relationship with God, from a dualistic consciousness to a qualified non-dualistic consciousness and from there to a non-dual consciousness. Then we could move in consciousness from a non-dual awareness to a qualified non-dual awareness and from there to dualistic awareness again, and thereafter, fluctuate from one consciousness to another as our life-experience unfolds. Our human consciousness oscilates between extreme dualism and extreme non-dualism. One can live from different levels of consciousness at the same time without any contradiction. It's an essential non-duality and functional duality. A useful metaphor could be a tree. The tree is essentially one, but functionally it has different parts such as leaves, branches, a trunk and roots. It is not necessary to hold any particular view on it. It is living in a dynamic relationship with God according to the need in our specific situations.

It is growing into the Love of God and Love of Neighbour

In IDM of Jesus Christ, the focus is on growing into the radical love of God and the radical love of neighbour. When Jesus said, "The Father and I are one" he was revealing the his radical love of God, his Fahter. When he said, "whatever you do for the least of my brothers and sisters that you do unto me" he was revealing his radical love of neighbour. These two are the two pillars of this monotheism. This is what constitutes the uniqueness of Jesus' IDM. One has to begin with the dualistic love of God and love of neighbour, and grow into the qualified non-dual love of God and love of neighbour and finally arrive at the non-dual love of God and love of neighbour. In a dualistic love of God, a person says: 'God is my creator, I am a creature and my neighbour is another creature of God.' In a qualified non-dual love, a person says: 'God is my Father, I am a manifestation of God and my neighbour is also another manifestation of God.' In a non-dual love of God, it is seen: 'Only God is. My Real self is God (aham brahma asmi) and the Real self of my neighbour is also God (tatvamasi).'—It is God loving God.

In the first level, our knowledge (jnana) of God is dualistic, our relationship (bhakti) with God and neighbour is dualistic and our actions (karma) towards our neighbours are dualistic. We are creatures and we love others as creatures of God. In the second level, our knowledge of God is of a qualified non-dualistic kind and our relationship with God and neighbour is qualified non-dualistic and our actions towards our neighbours are qualified non-dualistic. We are sons and daughters of God and we love our neighbours as our brothers and sisters. In the third level, our knowledge of God is non-dual and our relationship with God is non-dual and our actions towards our neighbours are non-dual. Here it is God loving God. In IDM of Jesus Christ jnana, bhakti and karma are not isolated but integrated in love. Love is not just devotion but wisdom manifesting in action. The purpose of every spiritual practice is to help us to expand our ego from the individual to the divine. The purpose of our human existence is to awaken to our unity with God and manifest that unity in our loving relationships.

Fully Human and Fully Divine

At the beginning we have said that all all philosophies, all ideologies, all scriptures, all religions and all prophets and sages tell us two important things: who we are and how we ought to live our lives in the world of time and space. Prophetic monotheism and the Dvaita (dualistic) system of Hinduism place emphasis on our separateness as human beings. They say we are mere creatures of God and remain always separate from God. Qualified non-dual monotheism, acintya bedabeda systems place emphasis on our divine son-ship and daughter-ship or servant-master relationship and close interconnection between God and human beings. We can have an experience of mutual indwelling—we in God and God in us. Non-dualistic monotheism and pure non-dualism emphasizes on our essential oneness with God. We can say that we and God are one. The first two have to do mainly with our humanity and the third one has to do mainly with divine sonship or duaghterhood. The last two deal with our divinity. The Dvaitadvaita system emphasizes both our divinity and humanness. According to this system at one pole we are divine and another pole we are also human. Christianity holds that Jesus Christ is fully human and fully divine but this experience is not possible for others. It is limited only to Jesus Christ. Jesus integrated these three levels of consciousness within himself. He was human in every sense, a true son of God and one with the Father. It is my opinion that Jesus Christ opened this possibility to every truth-seeker. Each one of us, whether he/she is conscious of it or not, is fully human and fully divine. Divinity, we could say, is our source and our human form is its manifestation or its vehicle. Divinity and humanity are intimately united in all of us. We also go through different experiences between these two poles. Our consciousness oscilates between our divine pole and human pole. Vedic Monotheism cannot be idneitified with any one particular system. It does not exclude any system but gives possibility to various interpretations but always transcends them. So also we can not identify the vision of Christ with any one particular system. Jesus Christ is not identical with any 'Christianism'. He does not exclude any system but gives possibility to different interpretations but always transcends them.

What differentiates the Integral Dynamic Monotheism of Jesus Christ from the Integral Dynamic Monotheism of Hinduism is the emphasis on the radical love of neighbour and the socially transformative action. Jesus died a violent death as he wanted to transform the society according to his vision of the kingdom of God. The Integral Dynamic Monotheism of Hinduism emphasizes very much on our love of God, on our vertical relationship with God. There was not much emphasis on the horizontal relationships and social transformation. The theories of karma and reincarnation have some how incapacitated these aspects. It is with Sri Ramakrishna and Swami Vivekananda that some attention was given to the poor and the social transformation. But today the situation is different. Many Hindu movements are involved in charitable works and socially transformative actions. Hence the difference between the vision of Jesus and that of Vedic tradition is very marginal. If these two visions can come together then more than half of the world would be united. What an astonishing thing to hope for? **Hence the Integral Dynamic Monotheism can be the meeting point between the vision of the Upanishads and the Bhagavat Gita and the vision of Jesus Christ.**

Sri Aurobindo spoke of breakthrough in the human consciousness and the descent of the spirit that transforms human consciousness and matter. For Christians this breakthrough took place in the person of Jesus Christ at the moment of his baptism and the spirit of God descended upon him like a dove and his whole being was transformed by the spirit of God. His transfiguration and resurrection were the signs of this transformation. Jesus said that 'the kingdom of God is like a woman who took yeast and put in three measures of meal until it was leavened'. Yeast is the symbol of the divine and flour is the symbol of human nature and matter. When God enters into the human and is fully received by a prepared consciousness then God transforms it completely. The human becomes divine and the divine becomes human. All our human actions become divine actions. Jesus said that "the actions that I do are not my own but the Father who dwells in me does his works". This is the work of transformation or divinization. For a Christian this is liberation or mukthi or salvation. It is freedom from our birth and death into the the life of God. Appearnace of every form is a birth of God and the discontinuity of every form is the death of God. In fact it is the end to our ego. If our ego is not there then every birth is the birth of God and every death is the death of God. The purpose of our human existence is to transform our life into the life of God and our actions into actions of God. Jesus said that 'the actions that I do are not my own but the Father who dwells in me does his works'. To realize our essential unity with God and live with wisdom and compassion in functional dualistic relationships in this world of time and space is, perhaps, the greatest miracle of life.

May all beings in the world be happy!

CHAPTER 2

THE TRUTH OF JESUS CHRIST

SANATHANA DHARMA AND THE KINGDOM OF GOD

I CAME TO BEAR WITNESS TO THE TRUTH

"May they all be one, just as, Father, you are in me and I am in you, so that they all may be in us so that they world may believe it was you who sent me" (Jn. 17.21)

'I came into the world to bear witness to the Truth' Jesus told Pilate. Pilate asked him 'what is truth? (Jn.18.37). 'What is truth' is the question that human mind asks again and again. What is the truth that Jesus came to reveal? What is the truth that Jesus came to bear witness? Jesus did not give any answer. He was silent. It may be the silence of someone who stands in front of an infinite ocean of truth and has no adequate words to describe it. It may be the silence of someone who knows that truth is something alive, something dynamic and that cannot be defined, that cannot be put into a box because to define the truth is to kill it.

It may be the silence of a modest person who knows that he is the embodiment of truth but hesitates to say it on the danger of being misunderstood or labelled as presumptuous. It may be the silence of a prudent person who considers that it is not an appropriate moment to speak. It may be the silence of someone who knows that the person who asked the question was not really interested to know truth and it will be a futile exercise to tell him about truth. Or it may be the silence of a loving and compassionate one who gives freedom to each one of us to complement this silence according to each person's growth and understanding of truth. One can speculate about this silence in so many ways. The author would like to propose that the truth that Jesus Christ revealed and bore witness is the kingdom of God.

Kingdom of God is Radical Love

Jesus did not define the kingdom of God but only described it in many ways. We can say that the kingdom of God is the experience of unconditional love of God. It is the realisation of the universal presence of God. It is the transformation of all our actions into actions of God. It is the realisation of the sacredness of creation. It is the experience of the radical love of God and the radical love of neighbour. Jesus invited everyone to grow into this radical love of God and love of neighbour. He experienced one hundred per cent love of God and one hundred per cent love of neighbour. In him the love of God and the love of neighbour have reached their climax, their limits and their fullness. When Jesus said, "The Father and I are one," (Jn10.30) he was revealing the radical love of God. When he said that "whatever you do to the least of my brothers and sisters that you do unto me", (Mt.25.40) he was revealing the radical love of neighbour. He is one with God and one with every human being and creation. In him the whole of humanity and creation are united. He is the kingdom of God. He is vasudhaiva kutumbakam. He prays for the unity of humanity and he lives for the welfare of the whole of creation: lokah samasta sukino bhavantu. "May they all be one, just as, Father, you are in me and I am in you, so that they all may be in us so that they world may believe it was you who sent me".

The Purpose of Revelation

The purpose of every revelation is to reveal who human beings are and how they have to live their lives in the world of time and space. Revelation is not something static but dynamic. The way God reveals to human beings depends also on their intellectual, psychological, scientific and emotional conditions. Revelation is not necessarily limited to that which comes from above but also can extend to that which comes from within hence also requiring the inner process of self-enquiry. It is common today to divide spiritual traditions into two categories: wisdom tradition and prophetic tradition. Religions like Hinduism, Buddhism, Jainism and Taoism belong to the wisdom tradition. Religions like Judaism, Christianity, Islam and Baha'i belong to the prophetic tradition. In the wisdom tradition revelation is something which human beings discover through their profound spiritual enquiry. In the wisdom religions there is a profound inner journey, inner conquest, inner purification and self-realization.

This process is guided by the inherent grace present in every human being. In the prophetic tradition revelation is something which God reveals to a person or persons directly or through an angel. Here grace is experienced as if coming from above, external. In the wisdom religions the focus is on interior liberation or self-realization. In the prophetic religions the focus is on the love of God and love of neighbour. Each way of understanding has its uniqueness but also its limitations. The ideal is the union of these two.

The author would like to propose that there are different levels and different types of revelation both in the wisdom and the prophetic traditions. These revelations are basically a continuous growth in divine-human relationship and human-human relationship. Here we shall speak of Hinduism as a model of wisdom tradition and Christianity as the sample of the prophetic tradition. Hinduism comes from the Vedic tradition and Christianity comes from the Biblical tradition.

Vedic Tradition

Vedic tradition is based on the Four Vedas, which are considered to be sacred scriptures of Hinduism. Upanishads are concluding portion of the Vedas hence they are often called Vedanta. The Vedas are considered to be eternal and without any human origin. They are called sruti. The seers or sages discovered them in their deep meditation. They are not understood as revealed, like the Commandments given by God to Moses on Mount Sinai. They are like the truths discovered by the scientists through their research. The only difference is that scientists look outside whereas seers look within. In the Vedas we discover that the divine-human relationship grew continuously and culminated in the Upanishads and integrated in the Bhagavat Gita.

The relationship between God and human beings was first expressed in nature worship in which natural powers like water, fire, air and sky are seen as divine. Human beings were completely dependent on them and they were at their mercy for their survival. Later this nature worship developed into polytheism when they began to personify the natural powers and worshipped them as persons. Water becomes AP or Varuna, fire becomes Agni, air becomes Vayu and sky becomes Indra, the god of the sky. This polytheism developed into henotheism in which one particular God became a kind of leader to other gods but not permanently but this position can be changed with other gods. Henotheism developed into monotheism in which one supreme God was affirmed: ekam sat vipra bahuthi vadanti, Self-Existing Being (God) is one but sages describe it by many names (Rig Veda 1-164-46). But their enquiry did not stop with monotheism. They went further in questioning the relationship of creation with that one God, as they did not accept the theory of creation out of nothing. They held that creation is not a creature of God but a manifestation of God. God is like a spider and creation is like the web that comes from the spider. Since creation comes from God it is sacred. They declared that everything is the manifestation of Brahman or God, sarvam khalvidham brahma.

Their search went still further and realized that the ground of human consciousness is ultimately one with God. Atman is Brahman. Atman and Brahman are synonym for God. Atman is the ground of human consciousness and Brahman is the ground of the universe. To discover Atman is to discover Brahman, because they are one. The journey is inside not outside. This experience is described with the famous statements like aham brahma asmi (I am Brahman) and tatvamasi (You are That, Brahman). This is the achievement of the Upanishad sages. This experience is often described as advaita—non-dualism. It means that Brahman (God) and creation are not two independent realities. Brahman is sat (real or eternal) and creation is a-sat (unreal or not eternal). Sat is that which exists by itself and a-sat is that whose existence is dependent on something else. God is sat and creation is a-sat because its existence is dependent on God. Some interpret this experience as monism in the sense that God alone is there and creation is an illusion. But the Upanishad sages were not monists but non-dualists. They did not use the word 'illusion' but a-sat, non eternal. It was Sankara who used the word 'mithya', which some translate as 'illusion'. In fact it is not possible to put Vedic seers in any particular system. They just communicated their experiences as they progressed in their spiritual evolution. The labels are given by others.

As human consciousness progressed the lower relationships were not rejected but allowed to exist as a kind of ladder to spiritual evolution. During the time of the Bhagavat Gita there were many spiritual paths and ideologies, sometimes in conflict with one another.

The author of the Bhagavat Gita was a spiritual genius as he was able to accommodate every spiritual path and ideology and proposed his own vision of Love in which the path of wisdom and action are united. He brought together human and divine, Arjuna and Krishna. Human will becomes a vehicle of divine will. Arjuna finally says 'thy will be done'. It was an extraordinary achievement and the work of grace. The impersonal God of the Upanishads becomes a personal God. A God who does not speak in the Upanishads speaks in the Bhagavat Gita. Krishna speaks non stop for eighteen chapters in the middle of the battlefield. Even though there is much emphasis on the love of God and selfless action, there is not much emphasis on the love of neighbour and socially transformative action. Since it was written in the context of battlefield its tone is very much focused on action that comes from wisdom. The external battle is taken as the symbol of inner spiritual battle in which there is a fight between the good (Pandavas) and the bad (Kauravas). Ultimately the good with the help of God (Krishna) wins the battle.

Three Theological Systems

Later three main theological systems were developed based on the teachings of the Upanishads, the Brahma Sutras and the Bhagavat Gita: Advaita, Visistaadvaita and Dvaita. The advaita system of Sankara affirmed the oneness of human soul ultimately with the divine (Jeevo Brahmaiva na parah) and it proposed the path of wisdom, jnana marga, for spiritual liberation; the visistaadvaita system of Ramanuja held that the creation and human souls are not identical with God but part of God or the body of God and proposed the path of surrender, bhakthi marga; and the dvaita system of Madhva held that creation and human souls are essentially different from God and proposed the path of devotion or surrender and action, bhakti marga and karma marga. The common element to these three systems is that they all believe that there is only one God or one absolute reality. Only dvaita system proposes God and creation as eternal but creation is not equal to God. In that sense they are monotheistic. So I would like to call advaita as non-dualistic monotheism, visistaadvaita as qualified non-dualistic monotheism and dvaita as dualistic monotheism. All these systems identify themselves as Hinduism. These three systems still hold their diverse views.

Biblical Tradition

Christianity comes from the Biblical tradition. We can also see a continuous growth in divine-human relationship in the Biblical tradition. In the Hebrew tradition the initial relationship with the sacred had been Totemism in which a particular clan associates with a particular animal (or plant), which becomes sacred and cannot be killed. Later it developed into polytheism in which there was the worship of many gods. Albert. C. Knudson says: "The sole godhead of Yahweh was a truth that was only gradually attained . . . . It was to Moses that the establishment of Yahweh worship was due. Previous to his time the Israelites seem to have been polytheists" Y.Kaufmann says, 'the Israelites were heirs to a religious tradition which can only have been polytheistic'. There was no direct jump from polytheism to monotheism but they had to pass through henotheism in which one God is presented as supreme over the other gods. H. Keith Beebe says 'it seems clear enough . . . that Moses was not a monotheist, yet to call him a polytheist seems inaccurate too. We can conclude that Moses stood somewhere between Totemism and monotheism. A term to describe this position is henotheism'. From henotheism developed monotheism in which the Hebrew prophets affirmed the existence of only one God and there are no other gods. Other gods were nothing but a dust on the scales. At this level God is the creator and human beings are creatures of God and there is a gulf between God and human beings. No one can see God and live. God reveals his will through the Commandments. The Torah becomes the will of God. The Hebrew prophets foresaw a further revelation in the future, a New Covenant, in which God will write the Law in the hearts of the people (Jer.31.31-34).

In Jesus Christ Hebrew monotheism grew into higher level of divine-human relationship. At the moment of his baptism Jesus transcended the prophetic monotheistic experience of God and realized himself as the Son of God. He is not a creature of God but the Son of God. He is the incarnation of God. The Hebrew tradition did not have words to describe this experience. It did not have any memory of that experience. Hebrew prophets used the words like 'New Covenant' 'New Heart, a Heart of flesh' 'New Jerusalem' and so on. This experience of Jesus was completely new to the Jewish tradition. It was the reason why Jewish religious leaders thought that Jesus was blaspheming. In this experience

Jesus inaugurated the New Covenant. He did not remain even at this stage but went further and realized that God and he were one. 'The Father and I are one' he declared. This statement also shocked the Jewish spiritual leaders. That was the last stage of his ascending journey. This experience is similar but not identical to that of the Upanishad statement aham Brahma asmi. Jesus did not remain on this level but descended again to his human level as he had his physical body and had to live in the world of time and space in human relationships.

If we use the Vedantic categories we can say that Jesus moved from dvaita (dualistic monotheism) to visistaadvaita (qualified non-dualistic monotheism) from there to advaita (non-dualistic monotheism). Dvaita is the experience of being essentially different from God. Visistaadvaita is the experience of being the son of God and advaita is the experience of being one with God. But in Jesus these three experiences were not exclusive of each other but were very well integrated. He is three in one: Sankara, Ramanuja and Madhva. It is the integration of these three experiences that makes Jesus experience of God original. He is Sankara in as much as he accepts the oneness of human consciousness with God (the Father and I are one). He is Ramanuja in as much as accepts that he is the Son of God or manifestation of God (I am in the Father and the Father is in me). He is Madhva in as much as he accepts that there is certain functional distance between God, creation and human beings (my Father is greater than me). Jesus is one with God, he is the Son of God and he is also a human being. He is fully human and fully divine. We cannot place Jesus in any one of these systems exclusively. We need to coin a new word. His experience can be described as Integral Dynamic Monotheism.

Revelation is not Static but Historical

We can see how in both traditions there had been an evolution of human consciousness from the lower level to the higher level. It seems that this evolution is similar. It is the marvellous work of divine grace. In the Vedic tradition it is from nature worship to non-dualism and from non-dualism it descends to qualified non-dualism of Ramanuja and then to dualism of Madhva. In the biblical tradition it is from polytheism to Christian non-dualism. In Jesus it moves from dualistic monotheism (my Father is greater than me) to qualified non-dualistic monotheism (I am in the Father and the Father is in me) and from qualified non-dualistic monotheism to non-dualistic monotheism(the Father and I are one). Then he had to descend back from non-dualism to qualified non-dualism and from qualified non-dualism to dualism. It means that the way we experience God and understand truth depends on which level we are. Revelation is not something static but dynamic. As we grow in our spiritual life our understanding of God and scripture also grows. In both traditions human consciousness has reached its highest level even though their approaches were different. In the Vedic tradition the journey had been through intellectual enquiry and interior growth to find one's true self or proper relationship with God, whereas in the Biblical tradition the journey has been through seeking the will of God in a personal relationship with God. The end result is similar but each is unique. Both are the work of grace.

The difference is that in the prophetic tradition as they moved higher levels they tended to be intolerant to the lower levels and even rejected them completely. There was, and still is, an attitude of exclusivity and intolerance towards others, though this attitude is changing in our times. In the Vedic tradition as the human consciousness grew into higher levels it did not reject the lower levels but allowed them to exist as a kind of preparation. There was, and still is, an attitude of inclusivity and much tolerance towards different beliefs, even though it is changing in our times. We need to grow in our relationship with God from lower stages of revelation into higher stages of revelation. We need to grow from dualistic monotheism (creator-creature relationship) to qualified non-dualistic monotheism (Father and son or daughter relationship) and from there to non-dualistic monotheism (God and I are one) and then we need to descend back to qualified non-dualistic monotheism and dualistic monotheism as long as we live in our physical body and live in the world of time and space.

Revelation and Unity

Some Christians think that Hinduism has only inspiration but not revelation. This position does not have any rational basis. Jesus Christ said: "the Father and I are one" and the Upanishad sages, five hundred years before Jesus, said, "God and I are one" (Atman is Brahman, Aham Brahmasmi). The Upanishad sages came to this realization through the illumination of their minds by the divine grace and Jesus came to the same experience through his personal relationship with God in the Biblical tradition. Both are the work of grace.

The Mission of Jesus: Not to Abolish but to Fulfil

Christians need to be aware that when Jesus said 'the Father and I are one' he was not telling something in built in the human consciousness in his tradition. This realization was already hinted in the Upanishads. The mission of Jesus was 'not to abolish the Law but to fulfil the Law'. This Law is not limited to the Jewish Law alone but to the entire spiritual realization of humanity until the time of Jesus. He did not come to abolish what went before him but to fulfil it, to add what is missing in it. We should look at Jesus as someone who is participating in the spiritual evolution of human consciousness. He is not making a solitary journey but making his journey as the representative of humanity. His discovery was the discovery of humanity. He integrated what went before him and added his own original contribution. He would have been very grateful to all the spiritual discoveries before him. The contribution of Jesus to his spiritual tradition was that he elevated the love of God and expanded the love of neighbour. He elevated the love of God from creator-creature relationship to 'God and I are one'. We can say that he elevated it from dualistic love to non-dualistic love. That was a revolution in his spiritual tradition. In this way he brought his spiritual tradition close to the Vedic tradition. His religious authorities could not accept that and considered his statements blasphemous. He also expanded the love of neighbour from the fellow Jew to every human being. He did this in the parable of the Good Samaritan. For Jesus the neighbours are not just human beings but also the whole of creation. He told his disciples to proclaim the good news to the whole of creation. In Jesus the love of God and the love of neighbour were one. His contribution, at that time, to the Vedic tradition would be to translate the radical love of God to the radical love of neighbour. In the Vedic tradition there was not much emphasis on the love of neighbour and socially transformative action. The theories of Karma and reincarnation some how incapacitated these aspects which were very much part of the vedic tradition.

Karma and Reincarnation

The Upanishad sages saw the fact or the reality of the relationship between cause and effect, action and reaction and the thought patterns that move from the past into the future. They called it karma and reincarnation. They realised that actions and thought patterns bound the human consciousness. They went beyond karma and reincarnation by realizing their oneness with Brahman or God. In this realization they were free from any belief including karma and reincarnation. Any belief creates a subtle ego. Where there is a belief there is an ego. Belief structures are a human need, like having a house for shelter, but they also create a subtle ego and thus become a source of conflict and violence. To realize our oneness with God is to go beyond ego, beyond all belief systems, and live from the inner freedom. Our individual consciousness becomes a vehicle of the divine. In this experience it is no longer we that live but God lives and acts in us. If our actions are God's actions then we are not bound by them. The Isa Upanishad says, "The actions done in God bind not the soul of a human being". Jesus said: 'the works which I do are not my own but the Father who dwells in me does his works'. It is the state without the ego. Later the fact or the reality of karma and reincarnation were made into theories and people were asked to believe in them. It is this belief of karma and reincarnation that incapacitated actions and social transformation. The Upanishad sages did not ask people to believe in karma and reincarnation and get stuck in this belief system but to see the fact or reality of them and then go beyond them.

Jesus' Revolutionary Answer

Jesus gave a revolutionary answer to the persons who asked him about a person who was born blind. Why is this person born blind? Is it because of his sin or sin of his ancestors? Their thinking was a kind of karma or reincarnation theory. It protects them from feeling guilty and responsible to that person. They can go home and sleep peacefully because they are not responsible for that person's condition. But Jesus said: 'this person is born blind not because of his sin or sin of his ancestors but to manifest the glory of God'. How can a blind person manifest the glory of God? Suppose the persons who are able to see have no theory and look at the blind person with openness, the blind person may awaken love and compassion in them and in return they might manifest love and compassion through their actions to the blind person. In this relationship, there is giving and receiving. The blind person sees God in the persons who are able to see and the persons who are able to see, see God in the blind person. They will be very thankful and grateful to the blind person because he has helped them to awaken the divine dormant in them. For both of them it is an experience of God. This is what it means that the blind person is born to manifest the glory of God. Jesus was telling them not to ask the question why this person was born blind but ask the question: how this encounter with the blind person can awaken the divine love within oneself. Awakening of love within oneself is awakening of God.

Giving and Receiving

The Biblical tradition says that the purpose of our human existence is to be 'fruitful and multiply'. This is not limited only to the physical level. It extends also to the other areas. To live is to relate. Human relationships are meant to experience divine in giving and receiving. They are meant to manifest divine attributes of love and compassion in our relationships. If we look at people as the manifestations of God, rather than as the products of karma and reincarnation, then our interactions completely change. It does not mean denying cause and effect and the consequence of past in the present. For example if a person smokes too much or drinks too much, this person may have the chances of getting cancer. The negative situations of others may help those who are in a better position to awaken the divine potentialities within them. The theories of karma and reincarnation may give some sense of security and stability to our minds that are confronted by the unexplainable events in the lives of the people and in the world around us but they also build walls around our hearts and make us insensitive to the conditions of others outside of us. They keep status quo and incapacitate our actions of social transformation. This is the subtle difference between the approach of Jesus and the approach of interpreters of Vedic tradition. Otherwise the vision of Vedic tradition and Jesus are almost similar. Thanks to God that the Hindu tradition has gone through a radical change in this aspect. It is also involved in charitable actions. Swami Vivekananda proposed to see God in the poor. He called the poor daridra narayana. Serving the poor is serving God. It is Matha Amrithananda Ma who said, 'if it is the karma of someone to fall into a pit, it is the karma of others to bring that person out of it'. We have to remember that the Indian sages always had an universal vision and wished the welfare of all. The expressions like vasudhaiva kutumbakam and lokah samasta sukino bhavantu bear witness to it. Of course there is always a possibility that people forget that vision.

The Contribution of Jesus

Two thousand years ago the contribution of Jesus to the spiritual evolution of humanity was that he elevated his tradition from dualistic love of God and love of neighbour to non-dualistic love of God and love of neighbour; and he brought down the non-dualistic love of God realized in the Vedic tradition to the non-dualistic love of neighbour. Truth is like a circle. Our journey is like a dot which begins at the centre of the circle and grows vertically and horizontally until it reaches the circle. Growing vertically is growing into the love of God and growing horizontally is growing towards the love of neighbour. It becomes a cross. Some people may be more attracted towards the vertical and some may be attracted more towards the horizontal. Some may stop on the way and may not reach the end of the circle. As human beings evolve there will be always some imbalances. The good news is that no one is outside this circle and no truth is outside of this circle. In the case of Jesus this journey was complete; it has reached its end, both vertically and horizontally.

The meaning of the Cross

This journey is the journey of dying to all the identities that separate us from God and one another and transform them into functional identities and not to have them as essential identities. It is breaking down all the barriers. Jesus died internally, before he died externally, to all the identities that separated him from God and others. He was one with God and one with every human being and every creature. In him the love of God and the love of neighbour have reached one hundred per cent. Thus the cross is the symbol of the fullness of truth and it represents the radical love of God and the radical of neighbour. But no religion, in as much as it is a belief structure, can contain this truth. Religions, like a nest, can only offer a platform where individuals can prepare for it. It is the responsibility of individuals to grow into this fullness of Truth and become the Way, the Truth and the Life. Only in the individuals this truth becomes alive, dynamic, creative and original. This realization also may become a mission in one's life, if that is the will of God, to help others to realize this truth. Jesus said, 'I am the way, the truth and the life and no one come to the Father except through me'. No one can come to the fullness of Truth that Jesus realized except the way through which he realized it. And his way was growing into the radical love of God and the radical love of neighbour. This is the only way for everyone. This truth and this way are not an invention of Jesus. They are there from all eternity. He only discovered them. If Jesus came only to tell humanity that he is the only Son of God and he is the only one who is one with God then he may have good news to himself but not to the rest of humanity. But Jesus came to proclaim the good news to the whole of humanity.

III

Six Types of Revelations

I would like to propose six types of revelations of God, not in an absolute sense, but tentatively through which human beings grow in their relationship with God.

The first level responds to the revelation of the God of history. It is the experience of God in time and space. This is the experience of God in the initial stages of human consciousness. This revelation may include Totemism, nature worship, polytheism and henotheism. Here the author has in mind particularly the God of Abraham, of Isaac and of Jacob. God manifested himself to Abraham, Isaac and Jacob and they responded to his call. They were the patriarchs of Jewish tradition. Here the relationship was very much personal. There was not yet an established religion with laws and structures.

The second type responds to the revelation of the transcendence of God. When Moses asked God his name, first God replied "I AM WHO I AM'. This is the revelation of the God of eternity who transcends time and space and who cannot be described with anything that is finite. The Jews were not allowed to make any image of God. Then God told him that he was the God of Abraham, Isaac and Jacob. This revelation was a very important one as it revealed that God has two aspects: eternal and historical. 'I AM WHO I AM' is eternal aspect and 'the God of Abraham, Isaac and Jacob' is the God of history. The Upanishads describe the Ultimate Reality or God by saying 'not this, not this', neti, neti.

The third type of revelation with God responds to the revelation of a Book or Commandments. God gave to Moses Ten Commandments in which he told Jewish people what they should and shouldn't do. The love of God and the love of neighbour are the essence of the Torah. The Torah became the word of God. Here we have the experience of the God of authority, who demands the obedience or submission of will and intellect and absolute loyalty. There is a gulf between God and his/her creatures. The holy book becomes the voice of God. It becomes the sacred scripture. To obey the holy book is to obey God. With the sacred scripture a formal religion, with its laws, rituals and authority, is established. This revelation creates a collective consciousness, a group consciousness, separating from the other groups.

The fourth type responds to the revelation of the limitations of the God of history and commandments. It is not a positive revelation but a negative revelation. Though God gave commandments to people their relationship with God osiclated between faithfulness and unfaithfulness. The majority of the people often broke the commandments and God sent the prophets to call them to come back to the Law. God also said to them that they were stiff necked and rebellious people. If the laws are not the self-understanding of the people but are imposed from outside there is always a possibility of breaking them. In the evolution of human consciousness there comes a stage where human beings feel that God is too authoritative and long for freedom from that authority. Human beings would like to have the freedom to think, to will and to act responsibly. As long as God existed human beings think that they cannot be free, as God has already determined what they should think, will and act. Here we have the 'death of God' philosophy. This 'death of God' refers to the God of history and not to the God of eternity. Agnosticism, Secularism and Atheism belong to this level. Though we may not call it a 'revelation' positively but still it purifies the revelation of the God of history and authority.

Atheism is a kind of fire that purifies the God of history. It shows the limitations of the images of God presented by religions. So we can call it as 'purifying revelation'. We should not look at it judgmentally but something that belongs to the evolutionary process of our human consciousness. It is not the final stage. If human beings are aware of the God of eternity from the beginning of their spiritual evolution then this revelation may not be necessary. It may take the form of Apophatic(negative) theology. Since some religions tend to make the revelation of God of history as absolute, this 'purifying revelation' seems to be a necessity. This revelation is a transition from the God of history to the God of eternity, from the God of authority to the God of freedom, from the God of words to the God of silence, from the truth outside to the truth within, from the way outside to the way inside.

The fifth type responds to the revelation of the New Covenant or universal mind. God promised Jewish people that he would establish a New Covenant in the future in which he would write the Law in the hearts of the people. From the least to the greatest everyone will know the Lord and there will be no need for one person to telling another to know God. God will forgive their sins and he will not remember their sins any more (Jer.31.31-34). In the New Covenant God does not reveal what people should do and shouldn't. God does not reveal a Book but 'who people are'. This revelation is also the revelation of the universal mind, in which a person is united with everyone and everything and whatever this person does to others he/she does to himself/herself. This is the experience of vasudhaiva kutumbakam, the whole world as one's family. Jesus said, 'whatever you wish others to do to you, you do to them. This is the Law and the prophets'. The entire Law is summarized into one: Love your neighbour as yourself'. In the universal mind a person does not strictly need a religion, a scripture and an authority. The reason is that for this person there are no others except God. He or she is all. This person has authority even over the sacred scripture. Jesus said, 'it is written in your Law but I say unto you'. He was greater than the scripture. At this level God will be experienced as indwelling presence, Emmanuel, as freedom and silence. Human beings will live from this inner wisdom and light and declare "I am the way, the truth and the life'.

Greatness and Humility

To say 'I am the way, the truth and the life' is a statement of greatness and also of humility. It is a statement of greatness because a person is completely free from the past and lives in the eternal present. This person does not follow anyone from the past but lives an original and creative life. This is also a statement of humility because this person does not become a way for others or to the future. He invites everyone to live the same way of life. He invites everyone to live in the eternal present. Jesus told to Nicodemus: 'the wind blows where it wills but you do not know from where it comes and you do not know to where it goes. It is like this the one who is born of the spirit.' It is freedom from the past and freedom from the future. It is to manifest the eternity of God here and now. It is the life of the kingdom of God. It is sanathana dharma, eternal religion. It is to be in the realm of originality and creativity in which no one enters the traces left by others and no one leaves the traces for others to follow. Everyone lives an original and creative life. Not to enter the traces left by others is greatness and not to leave traces for others is humility. 'No one tells the other to know God because everyone knows God'. This is the experience of the new covenant or universal mind.

It is Eternal Covenant

This new covenant is not really a new covenant but we can call it 'eternal covenant' as it is written in the hearts of human beings as they are born. God does not write anything newly but make them realize 'who they are' from all eternity. This is what happened to Jesus at the moment of his baptism. God did not give him any commandments, even the two great commandments, but he revealed who Jesus was: 'you are my beloved son'. This is the revelation of the eternal Word which is the source of all sacred books but no sacred book can exhaust it. With this God has said everything. In the New Testament God spoke only twice: at the moment of Jesus' baptism and then at his transfiguration but in both occasions he said the same thing: 'you are my beloved Son' and 'He is my beloved Son'. It is the revelation of the universal mind. Then God became silent because there was nothing more to say. This is writing the law in the hearts of the people or revealing the universal mind.

Return to the Garden of Eden

To discover the universal mind is to re-enter into the Garden of Eden. It is to discover one's original wholeness and fullness. It is to find the hidden treasure, to find the pearl of great value. It is to live in the universal presence of God. It is to walk with God in the cool of the evening. It is to go beyond fear of hell and greediness for heaven. It is to go beyond reward and punishment. The sacred books and the religions came after the fall of humanity. They came when human beings forgot their true self. They were not there in the beginning. A person who enters into the universal mind does not initiate a new religion, does not reveal a new book and does not become an authority for the others. His/her primary mission will be to invite everyone to discover the universal mind and live from there. He/she is only a messenger who brings the invitation from God to the humanity to enter into this new life. If he/she gives some precepts or initiates an organisation they are only meant to do what he/she did: to invite people into this new life and facilitate their growth, and nothing more. Jesus invited humanity to this new life with one word: repent. It is an invitation to enter into the universal mind, to re-enter into the Garden of Eden.

The sixth type of divine-human relation responds to human consciousness that one shares the divine nature. At this level a person declares, 'God and I are one', 'I am Brahman'. Jesus said, 'The Father and I are one'. This is the last stage in the ascending journey of our human consciousness. These statements need to be understood very carefully because there is always a danger of misinterpreting them, thinking that a human beings is God. The 'I' which says that 'God and I are one' is not an 'individual I' or 'collective I' or 'Universal I' but it is 'divine I'. It is God who says I am Brahman, I am God. Our human consciousness is like a bridge between the divine and our lower nature, body and mind. It is like a reflection of the divine in the mirror of body and mind complex. When this reflection identifies with the body and mind it feels like a creature but when it looks into its source, the divine, it says 'God and I are one'. Our human consciousness is the breath of God breathed into our earthen vessel. It is the seed of God in us having the potential to grow into the divine. We have said that in the fifth revelation human beings discover the universal consciousness. In the sixth revelation universal consciousness enters or grows into the divine consciousness. When it enters into the divine, the whole of humanity and the whole of creation enter into God. It is the experience of the whole of humanity and the whole of creation merging into God. The reflection realizes its source. It is as if the whole of creation has dissolved into God, as if it is the end of the world. It is going to the state before God manifested the creation. In this experience a person discovers the redemption of the whole of humanity and the whole of creation in the unconditional love of God. A person discovers the good news for the whole of humanity and the whole of creation. It is not the experience of a single individual even though the journey is happening in a particular physical individual. Jesus said, 'no one has ascended into heaven except the Son of Man who descended from heaven.' Jesus is the Son of Man, representing the whole of creation, in as much as he has descended from God. He is the manifestation of God. He also ascended into heaven and in him the whole of creation has returned to God. He is the saviour of the whole of humanity and of creation. (Salvation is not something new. It is realizing that we have been already saved by God. For God, creating and saving are not two actions. They are one. But we are in state of ignorance. We are not saved by any path or any person but every path or every enlightebed person helps us to realize that we are already saved by God.) This experience is like climbing the roof of a house. One cannot live there but has to descend again and integrate the lower levels, which are our human aspects, so that divinity and humanity are united and integrated. It is like a leaf whose awareness goes to the level of the roots and then it has to return to the level of the leaf. A person who realizes this truth becomes very humble because every human being has the same possibility but he or she is not aware of it. This person invites everyone to discover this truth and tries to facilitate that realization. This person may withdraw from the world or involve with the world according to the will of God that person feels within.

Human beings are not only rooted in divine in their ultimate level but also human as long as they are connected to their body and live in the world of time and space and in human relationships. Ascending humanity is elevated to divinity because descending divinity incarnates into humanity. It is divinized humanity. Jesus described this with a simple parable: 'the Kingdom of God is like a woman who took yeast and put in three measure of meal or flour until it was leavened'. The flour is our humanity and yeast is our divinity. Our humanity is divinized. Christians believe that Christ is fully divine and fully human. The consciousness of Jesus is like bridge between divinity and humanity. At one side he is divine and another side he is human. In him divinity and humanity are integrated. In this sense he becomes a way for people to move from humanity to divinity and from divinity to humanity.

The first three revelations belong to the God of history and the last two belong to the God of eternity. The fourth one is a transition from the God of history to the God of eternity. We can say that Jesus, at the moment of his baptism, moved from the God of history to the God of eternity, from the God of authority to the God of freedom, from the First Covenant to the New Covenant. Jesus declared: 'Before Abraham was I am'. He transcended the God of Abraham (history) and experienced unity with the God of 'I am who I am' (eternity). The Mundaka Upanishad speaks of two types of wisdom: para vidhya and apara vidhya, higher wisdom and lower wisdom. Lower wisdom belongs to the God of history and higher wisdom belongs to the God of eternity. We begin with the God of history and then we need to move into the God of eternity. These two are not exclusive. The God of eternity includes the God of history. We can say that the God of history is the womb of God in which God nourishes humanity before he/she gives birth to them into eternity.

Fullness of Revelation

The purpose of every revelation is to tell us who we are and how we have to live our lives in the world of time and space. The fullness of revelation is that which reveals that we are ultimately grounded in God. This is the radical love of God. It affirms divinity as our foundation and humanity as its manifestation. The fullness of revelation also reveals that we as manifestations of God, all of us need to live in loving relationships. Human life is relationship and in relationships we experience God. We need to see every human being as the manifestation of God and every creature as the manifestation of God and love them as such. We need to show special love and care to those who are most need it. 'Whatever you do to the least of my brothers and sisters that you do unto me' is the expression of the fullness of revelation regarding the love of neighbour. It is the radical love of neighbour.

Traditional Judaism and Islam focus very much on the revelation of the Book, the Torah and the Holy Koran. The entire focus is on the literal interpretations of the Holy Books. Human beings cannot go beyond the Book. This belongs to the third type of revelation. Here the love of God is dualistic, creator and creature relationship and the love of neighbour is also dualistic. Christians also generally reduces their revelation to the New Testament writings. Their love of God then is very dualistic.

According to these three prophetic religions human beings are primarily creatures of God. There is a gulf between God and human beings. Even after death human beings will be separate from God even if they exist in God's presence. There is no emptying of oneself in the divine. These religions deny human beings not only their divine son-ship and daughterhood but also their radical experience of God. Human beings are just creatures of God. The emphasis is on our humanness. The theory of creation out of nothing forbids the evolution of human consciousness into higher levels. Though this theory appears to be a satisfying theory it is not a very liberating theory since it keeps people eternally separate from God. It is rather a very oppressive theory. In Christianity an exception is made to Jesus Christ: he is a human being, the Son of God and one with God (Judaism and Islam do not accept Jesus as the Son of God or one with God, but he is just another human being. Hinduism has no difficulty in accepting that Jesus Christ is the incarnation of God and one with God but this is not unique to Jesus but a possibility to everyone). But in Christianity this possibility is limited only to Jesus Christ. He is seen as essentially different from the rest of human beings. And yet St. Paul insists that by grace we are 'in Christ' and St. Peter tells us that we 'share in the divine nature'. Mystical traditions of Judaism, Islam and Christianity have taken the human consciousness beyond dualistic monotheism to qualified non-dualistic monotheism and non-dualistic monotheism. In Christianity Meister Eckhart is a pioneer.

Integration of Human and Divine Aspects

The advaitic system of Hinduism holds that human soul is ultimately one with divine (Jeevo Brahmaiva Na parah). Only God is eternal (Brahma sathyam) and creation is unreal or an illusion (Jagat Mithya). The focus is entirely on our divinity. It melts our humanity with the ocean of divine. It tends to neglect our humanity. The visistadvaitic system of Hinduism holds that human beings are part of God, manifestations of God. God is qualified by human souls and creation. It rescues little bit of our humanness. Human beings can be sons and daughters of God and can have personal relationship with God. But they are not equal with divine. There is a subtle essential difference between God and human souls. It brings our humanity from the ocean of divine to the level of an iceberg. But it denies our divinity and humanness. The dvaita system of Madhva holds that human beings are essentially different from God, though not created by God. They are essentially and primarily creatures of God. The human consciousness is rather like the solid earth, different but bordering on the divine ocean. There is a gulf between God and human beings; this strengthens their distance and relationship. But it rather denies the possibility of realizing our divine son-ship and daughter-ship and also sharing in the divine nature. (It should be mentioned that the Hindu theological systems do not accept the theory of creation out of nothing.) Each system, by emphasizing on one aspect, neglects the other aspects. Only in the integration of these three aspects that human beings can have the fullness of revelation. It is the opinion of the author that in Jesus Christ this integration has taken place two thousand years ago and he opened this possibility to everyone. This is the good news of Jesus to humanity.

You Are the Light of the World

Jesus said: 'I am the light of the world' and 'You are the light of the world'. These two statements are the summary of Jesus' good news. They are the two sides of the same coin or two wheels of a cart. (One without the other is only half truth). But we are not aware of this truth. He invited humanity to discover this truth or to grow into this truth with the statement 'the kingdom of God is at hand, 'repent'. The entire message of Jesus is contained in this one word 'repent'. It is an invitation to people to the great banquet of the kingdom of God. The banquet is ready, please come and eat. It is an invitation to eat food at the divine table. It is the banquet where human nature is divinised and divine becomes human. It is the banquet where God offers himself/herself as a food and drink (of immortality) to human beings and human beings offer themselves to God as a food and drink, to be transformed into immortality. God eats us and we eat God. God drinks us and we drink God. It is the banquet of spiritual transformation, spiritual alchemy. We need to elevate our humanity towards divinity and bring down divinity towards our humanity. Our divine son-ship and daughter-ship is the bridge between our human pole and divine pole. It is the centre that holds these two, divine and human, aspects together.

Realizing Unity with God Makes One Humble

Realizing our divine foundation does not make us proud rather it makes us humble. Many people misunderstand the statement 'God and I are one'. They think it is an arrogant and blasphemous statement. On the face it appears like that. In fact it is the most humble statement anyone can make. It does not mean a human being becomes God. No human being can become God. If every human being becomes God then there will be billions of Gods in the world. There are no gods but

God. It only means to realize that God alone is and we all come from God and return to God. It may be wise to say, 'my true self is God' or 'my foundation is God' rather than saying 'God and I are one' or 'I am God'. Many people think that if we say 'we are the creatures of God' we are very humble. In fact we are not humble but very proud. It is a blasphemy. We are creating a reality separate from God. It is a sin because we have no separate existence apart from God. A Sufi master said: 'my own existence is my greatest sin'. It means thinking to having a separate existence apart from God. Jesus realized that he was one with God and then he washed the feet of his disciples. We can see the humility of a person who realized his unity with God. This is the uniqueness of Jesus. The deeper a person grows into God the more humble a person becomes. The virtue of humility is the sign of our spiritual maturity. It is possible that corruption can enter and people try to manipulate this experience for their self-glorification. When Jesus said 'the Father and I are one' the Jewish religious authorities misunderstood him. They thought he was blaspheming. In fact he was making a very humble statement.

Marriage of Wisdom and Action

In Christianity God spoke his final 'Word' through his Son (Heb.1.1-2). This final Word is the revelation of human consciousness being in the ultimate level one with divine consciousness. This revelation was not there in the Jewish tradition. The Jewish tradition foresaw the universal mind (the New Covenant) but not the oneness of human consciousness with divine consciousness. This revelation was already there in the Vedic tradition five hundred years before Jesus. The Upanishad sages had already realized this truth through their spiritual enquiry propelled by the grace of God. The originality of the revelation of Christ is the marriage of the radical love of God with the radical love of neighbour. It is the marriage of wisdom and action in love. Love is wisdom manifesting in action.

Jesus said that the queen of Sheba came to listen to the Wisdom of Solomon but someone greater than Solomon is here. The people of Nineveh listened to the voice of Prophet Jonah but someone greater than prophet Jonah is here'. Solomon was considered to be wise but his wisdom was dualistic wisdom. With all his wisdom Solomon could never have said 'the Father (God) and I are one'. Jesus said so. A prophet invites people to the love of neighbour, to the love of the poor, the orphans and widows. Jonah represented this love of neighbour. But this love was dualistic love. A neighbour is someone other than us. Jesus went beyond this dualistic love. His love was non-dualistic love: 'whatever you do to the least of my brothers and sisters that you do unto me'.

Non-dualistic Wisdom and Non-dualistic Action

In Jesus non-dualistic wisdom and non-dualistic action come together in love. It was the marriage of wisdom and action. This, we can say, is the fullness of truth and fullness of revelation that Jesus came to reveal and to bear witness. This is the kingdom of God. It is vasudhaiva kutumbakam; it is living in sanathana dharma. He invited his listeners to realize this truth. The religious authorities of his time were not ready for this truth, particularly the unity of human consciousness and divine consciousness in one person. They considered it blasphemous and Jesus had to be crucified for blasphemy. The crucifixion of Jesus was the consequence of Jesus standing by his spiritual realization and the refusal of Jewish spiritual authorities to accept his message and to grow in divine-human and human-human relationships. Jesus had to stand by his spiritual realization for the spiritual evolution of human consciousness even though he knew that it would cost his life. He accepted his death for the spiritual liberation of humanity. He had to lay down his life on the cross in order to open the door for the spiritual evolution of humanity, particularly of his spiritual tradition. Jesus died for spiritual growth, for unity, for liberation, particularly spiritual liberation. Even today whenever we refuse to grow in divine-human relationship and human-human relationships we are crucifying Jesus Christ. As per the radical love of God Jesus has nothing new to say to the Vedic tradition but his mission was to open this possibility in his Jewish tradition. His primary mission was not to reform his religion, not to give a new Book(in fact he did not write anything), not to start a new religion, but to inaugurate the new covenant, to inaugurate a new human consciousness, to inaugurate the universal mind, which can say like him, 'I am the way, the truth and the life'. It was to invite humanity to this new life. His message was a kind of spiritual revolution and also the fulfillment of the aspirations of his spiritual tradition. He tried to transform his religion to be a matrix for this new life. Since his religious authorities did not cooperate with his message Jesus had to form a group of his close disciples as a nest which can facilitate the birth of this new covenant, of new human consciousness, of universal mind. He gave them the keys of wisdom that open the door to the kingdom of God, the God of eternity. St. Paul said, 'if anyone is in Christ he or she is a new creation'.

The word 'Religion' means to re-link (humanity to God). A religion should be like a bridge that links the God of history with the God of eternity and through which people can cross over from the God of history to the God of eternity. People should pass over the bridge but not settle down on it, not to make it a living house. For Christians Jesus Christ is this bridge, he is the way. The spiritual leaders must be the experts of God of history and also established in the God of eternity so that they can guide people in their journey. If they sit on the bridge then neither they enter nor allow others to enter. They become an obstacle for the spiritual evolution of the people. In Hinduism a sage is described as someone who is well versed in the scriptures (srutistotra) and also established in Brahman (brahmanista). He/she is in touch with the God of history and also with the God of eternity so that he/she becomes a guide to the seekers of truth to cross over the bridge. The greatness of any religion does not consist in how many followers it has in its maternal womb but how many followers it has given birth to into the freedom of the kingdom of God. Jesus asked people (Nicodemus) to be born again. It is to come out of the womb of God of history and enter into the God of eternity. The gospel of Jesus is just an invitation to people to be born into this life. The conversion(metanoia) that Jesus intended was from the conditioned truth to the unconditioned truth, from the exclusive truth to the inclusive truth, from the fragmented truth to the fullness of truth. But unfortunately but understandably Christian tradition has made his unconditioned truth into conditioned truth and exclusive. (It would have been impossible for his disciples brought up in the exclusive Jewish tradition to understand the universal vision of Jesus.) It denied truth outside of its belief system. It interpreted conversion in the sense of converting people to its exclusive truth. This interpretation of Jesus' message does not do justice to the universal vision of Jesus. In fact it is just opposite of what Jesus intended. We have to say that Christianity is in the process of understanding Jesus' message. It is a long journey. Today it is by encountering other spiritual traditions its understanding of Jesus' message becomes enriched. The greatest need of Christianity today is to grow from its exclusive understanding of Jesus' message into an inclusive vision, where conversion is not understood from one conditioned truth to another conditioned truth, from one religion to another religion but from the conditioned truth to the unconditioned truth, from religions into the universal truth, into the kingdom of God, into vasudhaiva kutumbakam.

IV

The Challenge of Vedic Tradition and Christ of Vision

The Upanishad tradition emphasizes our divine pole where as the prophetic tradition emphasizes our human pole, our essential difference from God. In Jesus Christ a marriage took place between our divinity and our humanity. He is one hundred percent divine and one hundred percent human. He not only affirms divinity as the ground of our existence but also our functional difference with God. He opened this possibility to every human being. Christianity, with all its good intentions, limited this possibility only to Christ and closed the door (which Jesus had opened to everyone) to the Christians. One cannot find fault with it. In a tradition where the transcendence of God was emphasized it would have been difficult and impossible to the disciples of Jesus to imagine that they also can share the experience which Jesus had. But to accept the possibility of that experience at least to one person was a kind of progress. Unfortunately, but understandably, that understanding has created a kind of spiritual apartheid between Christ and Christians and gave institutional power and authority to those who represent Christ. Institutional power and authority have their purpose and value (in fact they are in the plan of God), as long as they are at the service of spiritual authority and power. Jesus told his listeners to obey the authority of those who sit on the seat of Moses. The power and the authority which Jesus gave to his disciples were spiritually liberating powers. 'Truth will make you free' Jesus declared.

Christianity is caught up between two positions: one per human beings and another per Christ. When it comes to human beings it holds the view of the prophetic tradition that human beings are creatures of God; when it comes to Christ it holds the position of Upanishad tradition that he is one with God. While

Vedic tradition (advatic) gives this possibility to every human being to realize one's divine ground, Christianity limits it only to Jesus Christ. This is the limitation of Christianity. The challenge of Upanishad tradition to Christianity is to open the experience of the radical love of God, which Jesus experienced, to every Christian and not limiting it to Jesus Christ alone. Unless Christianity opens this possibility it may be recognized in India for its social services and charitable works but it cannot appeal to the deepest spiritual aspirations of the Hindu heart and mind. In the same way the challenge of Christ's message to the Vedic tradition would be to translate its radical love of God into radical love of neighbour. It is to translate its wisdom into socially transformative action.

A Marginal Difference and Genuine Dialogue

The difference between the Vedic vision and the vision of Jesus Christ is very marginal. These two visions are similar regarding the radical love of God. They both emphasise the need to discover God as our ultimate ground. They are also similar regarding the need of human will becoming the vehicle of the divine will. Jesus said, 'I have not come to do my will but the will of him who sent me' and 'Father, if it is possible take away this cup from me, but not my will, let thy will be done'. Arjuna initially did not want to fight or act but then finally he says to Krishna, 'yes, I will do thy will'. They are also similar in as much as they both insist on the necessity of action. Life should manifest in action. Jesus said, 'my father is working and so I am also working'. Krishna tells Arjuna to follow his action of non-action. Arjuna has to act or fight. Jesus will not deny the process of karma and reincarnation but only his reaction to it would be different.

It is the genuine love of neighbour and the socially transformative action that distinguishes the vision of Jesus from the vision of Vedic sages and the Bhagavat Gita. It also changes the way one experiences God. Jesus presents a God, who is unconditional love. He does not sit above in the heavens and wait for the people to find him but he comes down to this world in search of lost humanity as a shepherd goes in search of his lost sheep. He does not come into the world in order to remove un-righteousness (adharma) and to establish righteousness (dharma) but to call the both righteous and the unrighteous into the kingdom of God that goes beyond moral righteousness and moral un-righteousness. He said, 'Unless your righteousness transcends that of the scribes and the Pharisees (morally righteous people) you cannot enter into the kingdom of heaven'. He admonished the scribes and the Pharisees saying that 'the sinners, the tax collectors and the prostitutes are entering the kingdom before them'. For Jesus spiritual life is not a battle between good and bad. It is not about righteous destroying the unrighteous but it is discovering the absolute good which transcends both the relative good and the relative bad. It is seeing the limitations of the relative good and seeing the possibilities for the relative bad. It is seeing both moral righteous and the moral unrighteous as the children of God. The purpose of incarnation is not to deliver the righteous and annihilate the unrighteous and establish righteousness (dharma) but to take human consciousness forward beyond the battle field between righteous and unrighteous into the unconditional love of God and peace. It is to change swords into ploughshares and spears into sickles.

Jesus presents God as loving and compassionate. He/she is close to the poor, to the sinners and broken hearted. He/she is at the service of humanity. He/she wishes to establish a just and equal society based on the values of the kingdom of God. Jesus had to die a violent death on the cross like a criminal as he tried to transform the society according to the vision of the radical love of God and radical love of neighbour. Today many Hindu movements have also opened to the love of neighbour and socially transformative action. Hence the difference between Vedic vision and Christ vision is very marginal. An open-hearted dialogue can bring these two religions together easily. If that happens, three billion people in the world will be united. What an exciting thing to hope for? To facilitate this dialogue Christianity needs to grow into the inclusive vision of Christ and recognize the grace of God manifested in the Vedic tradition.

V

Sathyam-Truth

In Chandogya Upanishad (8.3-5) there is an interesting analysis of the word for truth. The word for truth is sathyam divided as sat-ti-yam. Sat means that which is eternal, infinite. Ti means that which is temporal, non-eternal and finite. Yam means that which holds or binds these two, sat and ti, so it becomes sathyam. So truth is the union of the infinite and the finite, God and creation. But the infinite and finite are always united. They can never be separated. The finite can never exist without the support of the Infinite, like a tree that cannot exist without the support of the earth. It is our ignorance that makes us to see the infinite and finite as separate. It builds an artificial wall between them. When human beings become free from ignorance then they see the already existing unity between these two. The finite is seen as the manifestation of God, as the body and blood of God. So if, by fullness of revelation or truth, we mean the integration of humanity with divinity, the finite with the infinite, the temporal with the eternal then Christians can say that Jesus Christ is the fullness of truth, sathyam. In him the divinity and humanity, the infinite and the finite, the eternal and the temporal are united.

The description of Truth according to Chandogya Upanishad is very beautiful but it sounds being a very static description. Truth is not only unity of the infinite with the finite but also dynamic. It is manifesting in action, in relationships. In General the Upanishads propose the path of wisdom to self-realization in opposition to the path of action. The Isa Upanishad and the Bhagavat Gita add dynamism to this static description of Truth. The Isa Upanishad insists on the importance of wisdom manifesting in action. In the Bhagavat Gita Krishna guides Arjuna that the action should not be renounced but it should be done without expecting any reward. It should come from wisdom. The essence of the Bhagavat Gita is the marriage of wisdom and action in Love. To this dynamism of truth Jesus adds the aspect of love of neighbour and social transformation. For Jesus truth is unity manifesting in human relationships because life is relationships. It is the integration of the radical love of God with the radical love of neighbour. It is transforming our human actions into divine actions. This love of neighbour is not an obligation, not a compulsion, not a burden, not a result oriented, not to purify oneself and not to acquire merit, but a spontaneous expression that comes from the realization that we are all one in God. It comes from the inner freedom. It is meant to manifest the divine attributes in loving human relationships.

The love of neighbour does not mean just helping the poor and so on. First it is seeing everyone as the manifestations of God and relating with them as such and then helping those people who are in need physically, economically, socially, intellectually, politically, psychologically and spiritually. Ultimately it is helping people to find the kingdom of God, to experience the kingdom of God, to grow into vasudhaiva kutumbakam, one human family. It also means loving oneself. It is to love God as oneself and love the neighbour as oneself because we are all one in God. Jesus loved God as himself and he loved every human being and creation as himself. In the Isa Upanishad we read, 'A sage does not hurt himself by hurting others' because, for a sage, others do not exist. He or she is one with everyone. Jesus also said 'that whatever you do to the least of my brothers and sisters that you do to unto me'. The mystery of Trinity in Christianity may reveal that God or Truth is not static reality but dynamic reality. It is not a monad but dynamic intra relationship. It is unity and it is love. It reveals that life is relationship.

Eucharist and the Truth

Jesus revealed the essence of his truth through the celebration of the Eucharist. The Eucharist is the dynamic expression of Truth. It is the expression of the kingdom of God. It is the essence of the radical love of God and the radical love of neighbour. It is the realisation of the unity of the finite with the infinite. It is the transformation of the finite into infinite. The bread and wine represent the whole of creation and humanity. By elevating them Jesus transformed them into divine, into body and blood of God, into manifestations of God. In fact it is not really transforming them but seeing them already as manifestations of God because they are already the manifestation of God. It is not so much of elevating the bread and the wine but it is elevating one's own consciousness. It is our ignorance that veils us to see that truth. Jesus was free from ignorance so he was able to see the reality of creation as the manifestation of God. He realized himself as the body and blood of God. There are three ways we can look at the creation: dualistic, qualified non-dualistic and non-dualistic. From the dualistic point of view creation is essentially different from God. From the qualified non-dualistic point of view creation is the manifestation of God. It is the body and blood of God. There is a subtle difference between God and creation, they are not essentially one. From the non-dualistic point of view creation is essentially one with God but functionally different like energy and matter.

To Eat Jesus is to Enter into His Consciousness

The elevation of the bread and wine is elevating our human consciousness from the dualistic experience to the qualified non-dualistic experience and from there to the non-dualistic experience so that we discover that we are one with God at the source and we are also functionally manifestations of God. It is ascending from dualistic experience of God into qualified non-dualistic experience of God and from there into non-dualistic experience of God. This is the experience of the radical love of God. This is our ascending journey. Then he gave the bread and wine to his disciples and said: this is my body; take and eat. This is my blood, take and drink. This is the radical love of neighbour. This is his descending aspect. He had to come down from non-dualistic experience to the qualified non-dualistic experience and from there to dualism. He has to come back to the dualistic experience as long as he lived in the physical body and live in the world of time and space. He had to become food to his brothers and sisters. It is to give and receive in loving relationships. The Eucharist reveals that life is a celebration. It is a ritual, a liturgy, a sacrament. Jesus did not celebrate the Eucharist only at the last supper but his entire life, after his baptismal experience, was a continuous Eucharistic celebration. His whole life was a liturgy, a ritual, a celebration and a sacrament. His life was a life of fruitfulness and multiplication. The last supper was only an audio visual presentation of his life, his experience and his essential message before his departure from this world so that his disciples do not forget it. To eat the body and to drink the blood of Jesus is to enter into the consciousness of Jesus. It is to make our life also a continuous Eucharistic celebration. We become what we eat.

Do This in Memory of Me

Then Jesus said: do this in memory of me. We need to do what Jesus did. We need to celebrate this Eucharist. We need to elevate our human pole towards divine pole. That is to ascend from dualism to non-dualism. This is our radical love of God. Then we need to descend from non-dualism to dualism. This is our radical love of neighbour. We need to become body and blood to our brothers and sisters. Life is to give and to receive. It is breaking of the bread. The disciples going to Emmaus recognized Jesus in the breaking of the bread. So it is in the breaking of the bread, which is giving and receiving that we encounter Jesus, we celebrate the Eucharist. All our actions become a Eucharistic celebration. Our entire life becomes a Eucharistic celebration. The ultimate purpose of our human existence is to transform our actions into actions of God. It is to transform our life into the life of God. This is the real Eucharistic celebration. This is the coming of the kingdom of God. Jesus said, 'the works which I do are not my own but the Father who dwells in me does his works'. In Jesus, the kingdom of God was manifesting in its fullness. Every time when we say 'thy kingdom come', we are praying for the coming of the kingdom of God in our lives. Jesus said, 'first of all seek you the kingdom of God and its righteousness and all things will be given unto you'. The primary purpose of our human existence is to seek the will of God and surrender ourselves to God and allow God to live and work in us. Then it is the responsibility of God to provide all our needs.

Conclusion

Jesus came to reveal and bear witness to the truth. This truth is the kingdom of God. It is the good news. It is the experience of the unconditional love of God. It is the radical love of God and the radical love of neighbour. It is the experience of whole of humanity and the whole of creation as one family and living from that awareness. It is living in vasudhaiva kutumbakam and in sanathana dharma. No truth can go beyond that and no revelation can go beyond that. This truth cannot be defined into any belief structure or moral structure or into any philosophical system, theological system or political system. At the same time this truth does not exclude any person, any system of truth or any religion or any spiritual practice. The path of Jesus is one. It is the path of love: elevating our love of God and expanding our love of neighbour. This path is not exclusive. It embraces every path or practice that helps human beings to grow into love of God and love of neighbour. It is the path of growing from narrow individualism to the all embracing divine consciousness, the kingdom of God.

The truth of Jesus sees conditioned truth in every system. It embraces all concepts of truth and transcends all of them. It is like the infinite space in which people can build their houses (systems of truth) according their need and understanding but it transcends them all. All systems can act only as a platform from which human beings need to grow into it. Every system has some truth in it. A system is like a room with walls and a roof. There is space within these walls. It is because of this space that people can live in it. That space is a truth but it is a conditioned truth. If we make conditioned truth absolute then it becomes exclusive and also a source of violence and conflict in the world.

The kingdom of God is all inclusive. It is something alive and dynamic. It embodies in a person not in a system. It does not have a boundary. Jesus said that 'the foxes have their holes and the birds have their nests but the son of man has nowhere to lie down and rest'. He was living in the infinite truth, in sanathana dharma. Jesus also said that 'the kingdom of God is like a mustard seed. It is the smallest of all seeds but when it grows it becomes so big that the birds of the air will come and make their nests in it'. The kingdom of God is so big that it embraces all the conditioned truths (nests) that people construct but transcends them. It is the vasudhaiva kutumbakam; it is the family of entire humanity grounded in the divine. The conditioned truths are like nests which act as a preparatory ground to move into the freedom of the kingdom of God. If the conditioned truths are made absolute then they become cages in which people imprison themselves. Therefore we can say that in Jesus Christ we have the fullness of truth and the fullness of revelation. In him the love of God and the love of neighbour reached one hundred per cent. He was the personification of the kingdom of God, the radical love of God and the radical love of neighbour. These two are the criteria to evaluate every truth. Jesus invited his listeners to grow into this fullness of truth. He entrusted his disciples with the mission to realize this truth, to proclaim this truth and to bear witness to it.

POSTWORD

John Martin Sahajananada hails from Shantivanam which was the abode of enlightened men and seekers. He is the disciple of Swami Dhayaananda (Fr. Bede Griffiths) who was one of the great spiritual masters of this century. He inherits the spirit of these great men and enlightens the people through his writings and 04.00 p.m lectures in Saccidananda Ashram, Shantivanam. He is quite original in his thinking and is daring to explore the uncharted lines and areas in spirituality. He has so far published You are the light: a rediscovery of Eastern Jesus (2003) God is within you, discover: a parable of the Kingdom of God (2004), A brief comparative study of Sankara and Master Eckhart (2005), Jesus Christ a bridge to bring peace in the world (2006) The Four O clock talks : discussions with John Martin Sahajananda (2007) What do people say Jesus Christ is ? (2007) "Fully Human and Fully Divine: Integral Dynamic Monotheism" is his latest book. Though this theme appears in the form of one of the chapters in his book "What is Truth?", Published by ISPCK, New Delhi, 2012, he gives a greater depth and width to this subject in this book. Therefore the author presumes that you are familiar with his style and terminology and takes you into the depth of his thinking and vision. He begins with three most fundamentals questions in one's life: 1. Who is you? 2) What is the Life we are called to live? 3) What is the meaning and purpose of life? He looks for answers for these three basic questions in two categories of Spiritual traditions viz., Prophetic tradition (Judaism, Christianity, Islam and Baha'i") and Wisdom tradition (Hinduism, Buddhism, Jainism and Taoism). In his analysis he comes to the conclusion that in each tradition, though the religions are monotheistic, dynamic, they lack one thing: integration among them which makes them exclusive and falling short of their fullness. He goes one step further and says that these two major traditions need one another to discover their richness in dialoguing with one another and also challenging them to come out of their exclusivity and have an Integral vision. Then he defines Integral Dynamic Monotheism as a meeting point between Vedic vision and the vision of Jesus Christ; as an inclusive vision; and a vision that tries to integrate Prophetic Monotheism with Hindu Monotheism. Then he leads you through Vedic vision and vision of Jesus Christ to discover how they can come under "Integral Dynamic Monotheism". He gives us the keys to open the core experience of the seers in the Upanishads and Bhagavat Gita and Jesus's oneness with Father. These keys are found in the Chandogya Upanishad and Mandukya Upanishad in the form of the evolution of four levels of human consciousness. By using these keys, he lays bare the path of the human spirit in its quest for the absolute in Vedic vision and vision of Jesus Christ as he discovers the God of eternity. In this analysis he shows how Vedic vision, which is primarily to ascend to the higher level consciousness to realize one's oneness with God, attains a new dimension of the descending of the Spirit and divinization of human nature and matter in Bhagavad Gita, Sri Ramakrishna, Swami Vivekananda and Sri Aurobindo. Thus the latter thinkers in Hinduism corrected the lob-sided approach of ascending. When he opens the heart of Jesus which experienced the interchangeable oneness with God of eternity, he finds that to his surprise that Jesus had crossed, in his ultimate experience, the boundaries of dualistic religion and prophetic tradition entered into non-dualistic religion and wisdom tradition which is both shocking to the Jews and blasphemous to the Jewish authorities. Secondly Jesus had flung open to the humanity his non-dualistic experience with the Father to one all but Christianity later forced shut it by saying the he alone could achieve that experience of oneness with the Father. Thus Christianity as religion, unknowingly in her resolve to safeguard the unique experience of Jesus—the truth which was inclusive in its nature and essence, had reduced this great truth into a disputable exclusive concept. He says that the challenge of Upanishadic tradition to Christianity is open the experience of the radical love of God to all. In the same way the challenge of Christ to the Vedic tradition would be to translate its radical love of God into radical love of neighbour. Will Christianity open its eyes to see this great possibility that her bridegroom had given to it to become the mother of all creation? Will Vedic tradition recognize that it can become dynamic only the one who reached the top descends to his physical self to transform the creation that is in Him and he in that creation? It is a million dollar question. We do hope in the Spirit that is stirring the seeking hearts!

Rev. Fr. Devadoss, Holy Cross Fathers, Trichy.